ROMA WATERMAN

Roma Waterman
PO Box 825
Ringwood Victoria
Melbourne, Australia, 3134
roma@romawaterman.com
www.romawaterman.com

Published by : I was Carried Pty Ltd, Melbourne, Australia

This edition distributed in the UK and Europe by
Integrity Media Europe Ltd.
www.integrityeurope.com

Editing, Design and Typesetting by Sunset Digital Pty Ltd, Brisbane, Queensland.
www.sunsetdigital.com.au

Cover Design: Carl Butel at Deep Image.
www.deepimage.net.au

Management:
Anton Bekker
Head of Entertainment Business
LEWIS HOLDWAY LAWYERS
Phone: (+61 3) 9629 9629
Facsimile: (+61 3) 9629 9630
www.lewisholdway.com.au
antonb@lewisholdway.com.au

ISBN: 978-1-907080-25-8

Contents

Endorsements

This is a fantastic book for anyone wanting to walk with God and reflect Him in some way to this world. Roma has brought us some of the most insightful, inspiring and widely researched writing on the matter of our creativity. *The God Artist* will be a permanent member of my reference library.

Dr. Phil Pringle
Christian City Church, Oxford Falls
Melbourne, Australia

Roma Waterman is a dear friend and a great gift to the body of Christ. She has been worship pastoring, leading, singing, writing and ministering in our nation for many years and is highly respected among many prominent spiritual identities throughout Australia. Roma has a great ability to tell stories through her songs. She has touched countless lives and shares the great love of Jesus Christ through her music and by leading us into the presence of God. I have no hesitation in recommending Roma to minister at your event.

Darlene Zschech
Sydney, Australia

As a landscape photographer, I realised a long time ago that God's power and creative genius is visible in every created thing. So, it comes as no surprise to me to learn from Roma that God is in music too. Roma is a great musician, but more than that, she has a heart to help people locate and unleash their God-given creativity. People often ask me about the secret to my photography and I tell them that in order to take beautiful photos of creation you need to be in touch with the Creator. The thing I love about Roma's book is that she's giving out the same message. If you want to make beautiful art, get in touch with the creator of art—God.

Ken Duncan
Award-winning landscape panoramic photographer
New South Wales, Australia

Ted and Roma Waterman have been members in good standing at our church for the last 16 years.

Roma recently served for a three-year period as our worship pastor. As one of Australia's premier singer/songwriters in the Christian music industry, it has been a delight to pastor her. Her contribution to the life of the church has brought immense value. I have no hesitation in recommending her to you.

Peter McHugh
Senior minister
Christian City Church Whitehorse, Melbourne, Australia

Roma Waterman is a gifted musician, songwriter and worship leader who has an infectious passion for the Lord.

Brenton Brown
Songwriter/recording artist
Malibu, USA

I love this book. You can just see Roma's passionate heart for music and the creative soul dripping from every page. She has taken her God-given gift for inspiring others through music, combined it with her extensive knowledge of how a creative person thinks, and put it all together in a format that is a breeze to read. There is freshness here. Freshness that comes from years of dealing with the same mediocre and stereotypical view of creative people. She has combined an extensive knowledge of the origins of music and linked it beautifully to a relevant, God-inspired message for today.

Roma is incredibly well informed, brutally honest, passionate and humble. If you are anything like me—an artist struggling every day to define my calling, and battling constantly with blurred lines of ministry versus entertainment, relevance versus worldliness and ego versus God's heart—you will connect instantly with what Roma has to say.

I have always known that Roma was a wellspring of wisdom and inspiration—now everyone else will know too!

Michael Paynter
Sony Music songwriter/recording artist
Melbourne, Australia

I have known Roma Waterman for a number of years and have had the privilege of working with her at several conferences. She has great presence in the Holy Spirit. She knows how to wait within herself whilst she is leading people into an experience of rejoicing. She knows how to listen whilst worshipping. She has the capacity to touch people's hearts and lift them into a place of fellowship and worship with the Lord. She is anointed, passionate and sensitive to God and people. Roma is a great team player who served the purpose of our events really well.

Graham Cooke
Speaker/author
Future Training Institute, USA

Roma Waterman, through an intimate relationship with God and her years of experience as an artist, teaches us how to become a "God Artist" in her inspired new book. Roma's principles are spot on and provide us with a spiritual roadmap to discovering whom we are and what we were made for. *The God Artist*, loaded with scripture and practical thoughts. It could well become your handbook to finding your song and venturing into the deeper places where your destiny waits and your calling becomes crystal clear.

Rick Cua
Recording artist/songwriter
Former executive EMI Music Publishing
Nashville, USA

I believe Roma Waterman is a chosen vessel for releasing the new sound of the Lord in 'the Great Southland of the Holy Spirit.' Not only is she a gifted award-winning singer/songwriter, but she also possesses a sensitivity to the presence of God that is a contagious and all too rare component for this transformational assignment.

Roma utilizes the training method of Jesus—both in the doing and the telling—as she models presence-based worship and teaches profound biblical truths. She genuinely loves people and demonstrates authentic concern for their spiritual advancement. In this next season, I believe Roma will lead, influence, and mentor an army of spiritual worshippers that will overturn atmospheres and facilitate a strong habitation of God's presence and power.

Dan McCollam
Director/producer for Sounds of the Nations
and the Institute for Worship Arts Resources
USA

I have known Roma Waterman for almost 15 years. She is a seasoned performer and has a passion to see people encounter the love of God through her music. Aside from her musical talent, her integrity as a person is what sets her apart.

Henry Seeley
Planetshakers Ministries
Melbourne, Australia

I love this book and the glory it brings to the most enthralling and intelligent of Creators—the One who proficiently and affectionately fashioned YOU!

With her fascinating investigation into metaphysics, history and scripture, Roma Waterman unravels the spectacular elements of God the Great Artist, and what He has lovingly and deliberately imparted into His design for humankind—the gift of creativity.

Capturing the essence of our extravagant Father, Roma amplifies how He thrills in releasing His sons and daughters to freely express who they are by displaying their many hues of virtuosity and imagination as heartfelt demonstrations of worship, blessing and pleasure.

While exploring the spiritual inspiration, internal wellbeing and the practical applications of the God Artist, you will explore ever deeper the mesmerizing wonders of His heart and discover who you were created to be—The God Artist.

AJ Butel
Author of *Overshadowed*

Foreword

A time is coming and now is, when true worshipers will worship
the Father in spirit and in truth. Jesus Christ (John 4:23)

*T*he *God Artist* speaks to the new breed of artisans rising in the earth.
We live in an extravagant season of God-inspired creativity that dawns our
horizon as true worshipers are rediscovering what it truly means to worship
the Father in spirit and in truth. The God artists that Roma describes will
shatter the long-held stereotypes concerning creative people. Refusing to be
known as moody, difficult and unreliable, they will choose to tap the true
creative root as partakers and representatives of His divine nature.

I believe Roma's book will help the God artist realize the vital nature of their
role as a translator of transformational truths, and an architect of generational
mindsets. I applaud her research of historic examples that help artists see the
pathway of the great atmosphere creators, nation transformers, innovators and
reformers, functioning under a divine influence.

Many people speak a message; few become their message. I know Roma to
be a true God artist. She is a fiery yet compassionate person of faith who has
broken ranks with the status quo to take hold of a greater kingdom reality.
The pages of this book are loaded with her spiritual and practical insights that
guide the God artist deeper into the heart of God. From that place creativity
has no boundaries and ingenuity knows no limits.

The kingdom of heaven is at hand. The aesthetic kingdom is crying out for
its full redemption. Thanks Roma, for making both our artistic history and
creative destiny easier to grasp. *The God Artist* calls us up and out into a greater
inheritance in the earth, a richer relationship with the Father, and a deeper
expression and manifestation of our own creativity.

Dan McCollam
Director of Sounds of the Nations and
iWAR (Institute for Worship Arts Resources)

Acknowledgments

*M*any thanks to the friends and colleagues who have helped me during the writing of this book. Special thanks to Shellene Pillifeant; Lili Bragge for advice, cut and polishing; Anton Bekker for input, direction, friendship and for encouraging me all the way; Wynand de Kock from Tabor College and Tina Waldrom.

Sincere thanks to all my friends and family at CCC Whitehorse, Melbourne, Australia for always believing the best in me.

Grateful thanks to Sunset Digital for editing, typesetting . . . and the works. Gratitude also goes to my new friends at Integrity Music and Crusades for Christ in Asia and abroad.

Special thanks also to the Hooker, Keil, Marquis, Dench, Le Lievre, Moss and Lowrey families.

To my colleagues and friends around the world who took the time to read the book and write endorsements, I am humbled by your kind words and influenced by your contribution of Heaven on this earth.

Not forgetting Dan McCollam and Graham Cooke for encouraging words that help me grow bigger on the inside. Darlene Zschech, your input and friendship is a blessing to me. Thanks to all of you for always taking the time—it has marked my destiny profoundly and I am so grateful to you.

Finally, thank you to my amazing husband and best friend Ted, for giving me the space to write this book, for letting me read these chapters to you over and over again and allowing me to type on my laptop in the middle of the night without complaining! Your love and belief in me is astounding and beyond words, and allows me to be a better person. I love you more than ice cream!

This book is dedicated to my beautiful gift from Heaven—Angel. My daughter, may you always find the inspiration and courage to be the God artist that He has called you to be. Miracle child, I believe you were called to be born for such a time as this.

Roma

PART
ONE

Practical insights

Introduction

It is the creative potential itself in human beings
that is the image of God.[1] Mary Daly

*E*very one of us has been given a unique gift and a burning desire. The gift is the God-given ability of creativity. From the great inventors and those brave men who journeyed to the moon, to the songwriters who craft songs and capture the hearts of thousands—all of them have tapped into their originality to create something that helps both themselves and those around them.

The burning desire is to know the source of this creativity. The great artist Himself—God—has created His masterpiece of earth and mankind and allows humanity to draw from His creative wells. Regardless of whether a person searches for Him or not, the foundation for all creative greatness comes from God. Many pursue their dreams, their beliefs and their search for meaning, not realizing that their hunger is encouraged by a need for a relationship with the maker of all things. This is an ongoing quest for both believer and non-believer alike—because God is unfathomable and there is no end to learning who He is and how and what He has created. Discovering this is like having a bottomless treasure chest filled with the finest jewels.

When our unique gift to be creative is separated from our burning desire to know the Creator, we lose ourselves. We may still have the capacity to create beautiful things, but the source of all creativity becomes distant to us. Much like a heart attack victim whose blood flow to the heart is restricted, our creativity is minimized. The flow—the source—has been blocked. Yet what we create can still be beautiful. God does not change His mind when our creative gifts are used without Him because He gives gifts and callings *without repentance* (Romans 11:29). God gives freely to all men regardless of how they choose to live their lives.

Throughout history, there have been men and women who drove themselves to artistic greatness without God. Indeed, some of the greatest artists who have lived were not remotely interested in submitting to His greater power, yet they were hungry and abandoned to something greater than themselves—their gift. Eventually, the gift replaced the burning desire. It became worshipped. It became the master, and sometimes it even destroyed its carrier. The great man creates great things. His art lives on long after his death, as his own creation takes over and makes a way for itself. This is how powerful and terrifying the gift from God can be. It can destroy, or it can build according to its conduit.

For those whose heart was to serve the Creator rather than the creation, their contribution also lives on. The sounds of Bach and Mozart echo throughout history as do the great works of artisans who had no inclination to serve God. What makes them different is not the legacy of the works they leave, but what their art directs people to. Without being religious, people across the centuries combined their gift with a burning desire, leaving works that permeate culture with the fragrance of Heaven.

As we come to the end of this age, we are in danger of losing this. As modern popular culture infiltrates every corner of the world, we allow it to become our mentor, to teach and guide us as to what is an acceptable artistic pursuit and what is not. We reference what we do by how our respective industries operate: what is popular, what will make money. We are good at what we do, yet we embrace these parameters to create what we think are acceptable paradigms. We have lost the reference point—the axis—and the foundation of what it means to create with meaning. We should be drawing from a source that never runs out, and is greater than we are. Instead, our creativity is diminished, and we become shadows of what we could be.

This is what it means to be a God artist: to learn to be creative with God at our center. Somehow, we have subconsciously thought that to create things according to God's reference would be *too* religious, and not relevant or interesting enough. Yet in truth, it is the total opposite. To be a God artist means to be different; to sometimes be controversial, to raise the bar for others that come after us—to make history! We do not see this as much as we should because, supposedly, God-centered art is often looked upon as bland and ordinary; easy to digest by someone who has forgotten what real food tastes like.

I am by no means degrading pop culture. I am a product of it, and like many people, drawn to it. What I am challenging is the thought that for us to influence our culture, we need to be like it. We use it as our starting point to create, but like many who have gone before us, we should continue to model ourselves on something bigger and more powerful. We should be constantly challenging what we think it means to have God-centered art. Let's not settle for second best!

I pray this book equips you on your journey to greatness. My aim is to bring you knowledge from scripture and history, for with knowledge comes revelation and power, and most importantly, a relationship with our wonderful God. As we continue to learn, I pray that we will become more and more effective and imaginative in our artistic pursuits.

Let the God artist arise!

God as the great artist

God is the perfect poet.[2] Robert Browning
In the beginning God created ... Gen 1:1

Our God is the greatest artist who has ever existed. He created the heavens and the earth, and in everything He does, there is a masterpiece—even in something as simple as the way He explains things to his children.

The story of Abraham is the perfect example. His wife Sarah was a barren woman and well advanced in years when this poignant conversation with God was recorded:

> Gen 15:5 *Then He (God) took him outside and said, "Look at the sky. Count the stars. Can you do it? Count your descendants! You are going to have a big family, Abram!"*[3]

Often when God speaks, people experience revelation rather than just information. Instead of just being able to relay facts,

He is able to bring truth to our hearts and change us. I believe this happens because the Spirit of God knows exactly how to connect with our spirit. He knows what type of picture, image, song, scripture, circumstance, movie or television program will capture your attention. In His great desire to love you, He will use whatever creative expression He can to see you transformed and brought closer to Him.

Created in His image

I believe that it shows great creativity for God to permeate our lives in this manner. But let's take that notion even further. We are created in the image of God, therefore we are inherently creative too.

> Gen 1:27 *So God created man in His own image, in the image of God He created him; male and female He created them.*[4]

If we are created in His image, then we are also created to bring revelation through our art. It is through us that people may come to know Him; it is through our songs, dance, novels and paintings that people can be drawn into the supernatural world of the divine.

Now you might be saying to yourself something like, "Okay, there's no way my art does that! I've received letters of rejection for my novel from over 20 different publishers, so it does not seem to me that my art is making any difference at all."

It is easy to feel discouraged when we receive criticism for the efforts into which we have poured our heart and soul. May I suggest that if our art is not making a difference, maybe it is because we are defining success by the wrong measures, or have not understood the prototype of what a true artist looks like.

Success through our art does not often look how we expect it to be. The reason we do not reach our full creative potential is possibly because we do not often model ourselves on the great creator—God Himself. We look around us and try to be what we are inspired by, or what the current trend in our society accepts as great art. There is nothing wrong with learning from our mentors, or being taught a craft by skilled teachers, but to be true to what God has placed on the inside of us, we must first and foremost look to Him. Yet we often do this as the last resort—when nothing else has worked and there are no further options.

We can learn to be at the peak of our creativity by understanding the marvelous creativity of God. Because we are made in His image, He is our role model. Why not learn from the source?

Why did God create?

> Is 43:7 *Everyone who is called by My name, whom I created for My glory, whom I formed and made.*[5]

It is clear from this verse alone that God created mankind for His glory.

The word glory here comes from the Hebrew word "Kabowd." Other meanings for this word include "honor," "glorious," "abundance," "dignity," "reverence," and "reputation."[6]

If we are to take this verse literally, God created not only the heavens and the earth, but *you*—for His reputation! For his honor! That means you are better than you think you are. His motive in creating you reveals His character—abundant and glorious!

Great art witnesses of God

It is thought-provoking to consider that all His handiwork witnesses of Him. Even when He does not speak with His voice, His art declares who He is.

If we are to model ourselves after the great Creator then our art must glorify God. Without words, our art should speak of His glory. It should speak of His abundance, His honor, His reverence. How awe-inspiring it would be to create a work of art that shows a person exactly who God is even though that person has no experience of God. Your work could be a testimony of salvation to a lost person.

In 1 Kings 6 and 7, the building of Solomon's temple is described in detail. It was a majestic and beautiful structure. Historians suggest it was one of the most beautiful buildings ever created. It was fit for the King of Kings. It was built to strategic specifications, and only the best materials were used. The temple was a testament to all of the majesty and greatness of a rich and powerful God.

To build something that witnessed so powerfully meant several things needed to occur. First, King David (Solomon's father), and Solomon, needed to communicate with God for specifications and instructions on exactly how to build the temple. Second, it took time. Seven years to be exact (1 Kings 6:38). Just like David and Solomon, we also need to listen to what God is trying to say, and it is okay if it takes a little while. That is what it may take to create lasting works of art.

David had many spoils of war from his years of battle that had been stored and were eventually used in the building of the temple. There was so much gold and silver that no one could keep a record of exactly how much there was.[7]

There is also much gold and silver that comes from the trials we face in our own lives; more than we could ever record. We should never underestimate what we have come through, and that it can build something in our future that is priceless. None of our trials are wasted—there is truth in the words of Keith Green's song, that our *trials turn to gold*."[8]

There are many other scriptures in the Bible where art

witnesses of and to God. Here are a few of them for you to ponder:

> **IN SONG:**
> Sam 22:50 *Therefore I will praise you, O LORD, among the nations, I will sing praises to Your name.*[NIV]

> **IN DANCE:**
> Psalm 149:3 *Let them praise His name with dancing and make music with tambourine and harp.*[NIV]

> **IN CREATION ITSELF:**
> Genesis 15:5 *He took him outside and said "Look up at the heavens and count the stars—if indeed you can count them." Then He said to him, "So shall your offspring be."*[NIV]

All art glorifies something

No matter what form of artistic expression, ALL art glorifies something or someone. I believe creativity is a truly spiritual experience, and so when people create, it can become twisted and glorify dark things, or even ourselves. Some people consider this kind of art to be beautiful, and this is because they have never truly experienced the revelation of "God-centered art."

It is important that you find the true gift that is within you and be faithful in creating from the truth that has been given to you. It will witness of and to God and can change people's lives, and even their eternal destinies. Do not think that this means you need to sing in church, or that you need to be in full-time ministry. One of the biggest mistakes we can make is to think that if we want to glorify God we must create something "religious." If you are a Christian, then no matter what vocation you are called to, it can be your forum for great artistic expression that points you to Heaven.

It is a good habit to regularly ask yourself if your art glorifies God. Be bold enough to ask yourself questions when you are creating. How does it make you feel when you experience it? (A song, a dance, reading a chapter of prose or poetry that you have just written, for example). Are you inspired? Encouraged? Or do you feel heavy, depressed and weighed down?

It is not wrong to create honest works from a place of emotional turmoil. Many artistic people lean toward feelings of melancholy, and only believe they can create great work when things are tough. King David wrote many Psalms that were heartfelt and painful as he cried out to the Lord for His mercy and intervention. What is unhealthy is if it is a regular condition of the heart. If we look back over the centuries, all great artists have had seasons in their lives when they created during dark times. But it should never drag you or others down; it should never keep you in the same place. Allow your difficult moments to bring you to a place where, like King David, you can experience the goodness and mercy of a loving God, who has a future and a hope for you.

I know that some of my best songs are those I have written when I was struggling with something. Nevertheless, at the end of writing them I felt encouraged and strengthened. I urge you always to go to a place of hope, even in your toughest times. This does not mean that every thing you create needs to be "happy-clappy." There is a spirit that will permeate everything you do if you always determine to have inner hope. Even when you create something that expresses hardship or sorrow, regardless of the topic or theme, there can be an air of grace and mercy that runs through it.

It is easy to let your emotions dictate where your art will go, but it is your art that should dictate where your emotions will go. Author Madeline L'Engle often talks about "serving the work, not the work serving you." You will be surprised at what can come out of you when you allow the creative Spirit of God to guide you. Sometimes this can feel as if you are going against your own emotions, but being led by His spirit goes higher and deeper than that. I guarantee that you will create something that is of lasting value that will not only bless others, but will also bless and teach you in the process.

Great art has meaning

Just as God created the earth to be inhabited by people, we can create our art to be inhabited by God. If we are created in the image of God, then we were also born to create, like God. It could also mean that your creation is not in vain—it was formed to be inhabited and to have life.

> Isa 45:18 *For this is what the LORD says—He who created the heavens, He is God; He who fashioned and made the earth, He founded it; He did not create it to be empty, but formed it to be inhabited—He says: "I am the LORD, and there is no other."*NIV

The purpose of your art is to bring blessing to others, to have movement—it is not dead, but can represent the life and breath of God.

Great art is meaningful. It makes people think. It moves people. God created so many beautiful things. The peacock. The hippopotamus. A sunrise. Fireflies. But His greatest work of art is YOU. Your life has meaning and is of great worth!

> Eph 2:10 *For we are God's workmanship, created in Christ Jesus to do good works, which God prepared in advance for us to do.*NIV

Great art needs the right environment

However, before God created His greatest masterpiece (You), He needed to create the right environment. He created the animals, the land, the water—a place where His greatest creation could survive. It is the same with our gifts. Before you begin to write the greatest novel, that hit song, or paint a masterpiece, ask yourself what environment you have set up for it.

You need to create an environment that allows your gifts to thrive so that you can create sustainable things—things that last. How do you do this? I believe the most important way to achieve this is found in this scripture:

Mt 6:33 **But seek first His kingdom and His righteousness, and all these things will be given to you as well.**[NIV]

To seek first God's Kingdom is to always be seeking out what He wants. There are many ways we can do this. By finding a church where we feel part of a family and hear great practical teaching for our lives. By seeking out mentors who can advise us. By making good friends who will lend a listening ear and make the journey of life with us. By regular prayer time, reading good books, finding time to rest and giving God room to speak personally to us. By living a life from a place of humility rather than one of self-promotion and self-gratification.

Time to rest

If you are like most people, you never have enough time to do all the things you really need to do. It seems as though there is never enough time in the day to get everything done. Throw into the mix having children, working, church life, sickness, a death in the family or running a business—whatever the constraints and demands, life can sometimes feel out of sync. Sometimes I have to force myself to take a break. I am always thinking of things I should have done when it comes to bedtime! The greatest challenge for all of us can be finding time to rest.

I am humbled by the thought that when God created the

heavens and the earth, as stated in Genesis, on the seventh day He rested. If God as the great artist rested after His work, then I should be modelling myself on Him.

If we progress with this thought even further, there was a reason that God could rest. It was because what He created was so marvellous, so glorious and so perfect, *that it continued to be creative* even when God was at rest. He created a work that could continue to create itself.

Think of the human body. It is created to regenerate itself. Fifty thousand of the cells in your body will die and be replaced with new cells, all while you have been reading this sentence![9] (That accounts for one billion cells every hour.) Did you know your ears and nose continue to grow throughout your entire life?[10] (Not good news for some people!) In fact, the tooth is the only part of the human body that cannot repair itself. If a person has two-thirds of their liver removed from trauma or surgery, it will grow back to its original size in four weeks.

The earth is also alive and evolving—NASA scientists have estimated that the universe will most likely expand forever at an ever-increasing rate.[11] It is incredible to think that thousands of years ago God created the heavens and the earth, and yet today it continues to grow and expand. If we tried to count the stars in our galaxy at a rate of one per second, it would take us 2500 thousand years to count them all. This does not even take into account the new stars that are constantly being formed, which means we can never count them all![12]

God was able to rest because he created something so spectacular that it is relevant and working today and continues to be creative for eternity.

Most business people will tell you the best products to invent are the ones that sell themselves. Somewhere around the world someone is buying that latest product. Without even realizing it, they are following the model of the great artist—if you create something great, it will last, and will continue to create itself even when you are at rest.

Rest = Recharge

If you take time to create something of lasting value, and if you take time to rest, you can continue to create at a high level throughout your whole lifetime.

It gives you time to reflect. To admire your work. To recharge your batteries. I often find when I take a break I have more room for creative ideas and they tend to come much quicker than I expected. This is because I've allowed God room to speak to me, and I've created space for Him to speak.

When you create something special, it has lasting value. It witnesses to and of God, and it is appreciated not just for a moment, but for a long time—sometimes even centuries. Today we still experience the music of Mozart, the paintings by Van Gogh, the wonder of cars and aeroplanes. Do you want to be that kind of artist? Follow God's example and you will be.

3

The artist and discipline

If I leave my work for a day, it leaves me for three.[13]
Madeline L'Engle

David was young and talented. It seemed as if he could play any instrument he decided to pick up and was a very good songwriter. His dream was to "make it big" in the music industry. When he was growing up, he attended church regularly but these days he did not get involved unless it was for a special event.

"If you keep working on your song writing you could be one of the best songwriters in the country," one industry professional had told him. In fact, record labels were keeping their eye on him. He wanted to make sure he had time to develop his writing so he took a part-time job and rarely took part in church activities.

David was excited, and for a few months he would diligently sit down with every intention of writing the next hit song.

But he would become distracted by everyday chores—answering the phone, checking his emails, going to the local store—and the creative juices just would not flow.

Three years passed, and David had written some bits and pieces that displayed his undoubted potential, but he lacked the discipline to follow through to expand and refine his songs. Eventually, the record companies gave up waiting for him to deliver, and they invested in other artists who were prepared to give more time to their work. In the end, David became bitter and frustrated, and gave up his idea of being a great songwriter. He never achieved his dream.

Unfortunately, this is a story I hear all too often. There are so many people who have a dream, but lack the discipline to take it further. Many of these people are incredibly gifted, and with the right attitude and discipline to work on their craft, could really thrive.

I've had times where I have not been disciplined. It is a constant struggle in some areas in my life and there will always be things I will have to work on. This is why discipline is so important, because there will always be an area where I can improve.

Creative people tend to be driven by inspiration and ideas; the word "discipline" does not fit comfortably with us. I've certainly had moments when I have written songs that came to me quickly—moments of inspiration. I love those moments, but if I only wrote a song, or only ministered when I was "inspired," I would only do so two or three times a year!

Let me share an amazing thought with you. Discipline breeds creativity. It is the water for the soil of your gift. It is not easy to include structure in your life, especially when you may not be an organized person. However, when you do achieve discipline, you will find treasures deep inside you that you never even knew existed.

This is because discipline forces you to dig deeper than just below the surface. I once heard a great songwriter say that it takes five minutes to *write* a song, and about three months to *refine* a song. Another great saying is: "A diamond is just a piece of coal that stayed on the job."[14] What you have inside of you is precious, and if you allow yourself the time and energy to work on your innate gifts, you will create precious jewels that can be admired not only by yourself, but by other people too.

Imagine walking into someone's home and smelling the beautiful aroma of a cooked roast. It smells great, but it does not compare to actually eating it. Most of us live our lives smelling the roast without ever actually tasting it! We think it is great because it smells so good, but we are missing out. Your creativity is a precious thing. However, if you do not develop it and discipline yourself to delve deeper, all you have is that beautiful aroma, and that won't be enough to fulfil and satisfy you for a lifetime.

Discipline will not come easy. You will hate it at times. You will become frustrated, and wonder if you are really doing what God has called you to do because it seems too hard. But it's all part of God's plan to allow your gifts to flourish and grow.

There are many things that can prevent you from living a disciplined life and there are also some practical things you can put in place that will help you. Let's explore some of these together.

Self-talk

For many years people thought I was a confident person because I was so outgoing. But the way I saw myself was quite the opposite. After a few difficult seasons, I began to realize that my attitude was changing. I did not have the best self-image and I was always feeling as if I never quite measured up to people's expectations of me.

The cause of my poor self-image was due to my lack of personal time with God, and my self-talk. We all have them—conversations you have with yourself in your head. The ones you have when you are trying to sort things out in your mind. Some people call it their "internal dialogue."

Self-talk is a powerful thing. It not only changes your whole perception of how you see yourself, but also how you perceive your circumstances. A good example of this is the story of the girl who walks into a room full of people who are talking. When she enters, they immediately stop talking. Depending on how she sees herself and others, she might adopt a negative view that suggests they were gossiping about her. On the other hand, a positive view might suggest that they were planning her surprise birthday party!

> Romans 12:2 *Do not conform any longer to the pattern of this world, but be transformed by the renewing of your mind. Then you will be able to test and approve what God's will is—His good, pleasing and perfect will.*[15]

To be transformed, we need a renewing of the mind. The scripture says "renewing" rather than "renewed" because it gives the impression that it is an ongoing event—which is true. The pattern of this world can often be to think the worst of people and of yourself. But for us to be truly changed, we need to renew our mind. One way to do this is to change your internal dialogue.

About ten years ago, I was very sick. I was told that I may never sing again and that I was in a poor state of health. Some days, I could not get out of bed. You can probably guess my self-talk was not very good. I lost confidence and hated my life. I then started to spend time with the Lord and I realized He wanted me to change the way I saw myself. I needed a new frame of mind.

I decided to read the Bible and I wrote down scriptures about my health and how God sees me. These scriptures would lift me up out of the dark place I was in. I put the scriptures into a prayer and every morning I would stand in front of the mirror and pray. I would tell myself that I was worth something, that God wanted me to be healthy, that I was precious to Him.

It totally transformed me, and made me feel so much better about myself, because I was beginning to see myself the way God sees me. I am totally healed today, and I have never forgotten what a significant part renewing my mind has played in allowing the Lord to heal me from within. What I was doing was aligning myself with God's heart, which was much healthier than my own. Eventually His ways began to influence me, until I was *transformed* by His words.

Why not stop for a moment and listen to your heart? How do you see yourself? Is there a common thought or phrase that you constantly recant in your mind? Maybe you feel that you're not good at anything, not pretty/handsome enough, too fat or too skinny—stop those thoughts right now in Jesus' name! Start saying to yourself that you are precious because God made you. You might make mistakes, but you are accepted and loved, and He has a huge future for you. You will be amazed at the freedom you will experience.

The other part of Romans 12:2 that I love is: *Then you will be able to test and approve what God's will is.*[16] This is an amazing thought. When our mind is transformed, we will have a clearer understanding of what the will of God is for our lives. This is because we will see circumstances in light of the truth—we will see things for what they really are, not what we *think* they are. We will not only have a truthful view of the circumstances around us, we will be able to deal with them with the wisdom of God, not simply by our own perceptions or wisdom. Life is not always going to be easy, but changing what is happening within us, can bring a greater clarity and truth to every situation.

Discouragement

Something else that can prevent us from becoming disciplined is when we are discouraged. This is something I have had to deal with in my own life. When I was younger, many people would tell me what I was doing wrong in my career. I often felt as if I was being examined every time I worked hard at something. I became unsure of what I was meant to do because I was weak in my faith and did not have confidence in what God had called me to do. Most people mean well, but when you feel you have put in a great deal of effort with something in your life and you are constantly feeling that it is never quite good enough, it is easy to abandon ship and start working towards something else.

Have you ever felt like that? Have you ever had a dream to do something, only to be told that you can't do it, that you are not talented enough, and that you do not have the right personality? All those things can make you pack up your dreams and lock them away.

Overcoming discouragement is possible. It starts with what we have previously mentioned, by having a real relationship with God and being transformed by the renewing of our mind. The next step is ensuring the right people are speaking into your life. When we have the right people around us, even negative feedback can be turned into a positive experience. This is because comments and suggestions will be made out of love and care for you, rather than jealousy or resentment.

In my early years of ministry I thought a "servant heart" meant I needed to take on board everything everyone said to me. I often became confused and discouraged because there were too many voices in my life. Some people would take opposing views, and I would become confused and frustrated. I realized

that I was being unwise in allowing so many people to influ
my life.

To be truly encouraged, it is important to have the right
friends and mentors around you. People who will not be afraid
to tell you the truth, who will encourage you, and give you a
shoulder to cry on when you need it. People who will let you
be yourself!

However, this type of encouragement will probably only
come from a few trusted voices in your life. If someone is mentoring you, do not be afraid to be completely honest with them.
Also, expect healthy mentoring to occur even when times are
tough. Sometimes you may not hear from a mentor what you
want to hear. You are going to experience difficult situations
where, dare I say it, *you* may even be the problem! (I'm speaking from experience here as I've been the problem many times!)
Do not run from this. It is valuable and if you demonstrate resil-
ience, you will thrive. Keep your heart soft and be willing to
grow and change.

Spending time with God

You've probably gathered by now that the basis for creativity in
its purest sense stems from an intimate relationship with God.
It is easy to go to people to find the advice and solace you need
but ultimately that can only come from God. When we have
a personal relationship with Him, we can weather the storms
much better because we know He is on our side. Even though
it is important to accept the support of those around you—HE
will encourage you more than any person can. Jesus says:

> John 14:26 *But the Counsellor, the Holy Spirit, whom the
> Father will send in my name, will teach you all things and
> will remind you of everything I have said to you.*[17]

The Holy Spirit as the comforter is a great image. Many

translations call the Holy Spirit the comforter. Comforter means "a helper or an assistant." I always imagine that means the Holy Spirit is saying to me: "You are awesome! Do not forget what your God says about you! Keep hanging in there, you are doing great things! We love you! We are your biggest fans!"

You have constant, divine encouragement on hand with you wherever you go, in the form of the wonderful Holy Spirit. You will find it easier to hear his voice if you are spending regular time with the Lord.

Too many distractions

At the beginning of this chapter, you will have read in the story about our friend David having many distractions in his life. This made it difficult for him to stay focused on song writing.

There are some everyday events in our lives over which we have no control, but there are some things that we can control and that we can eliminate from our lives.

When our lives are hectic, we become distracted instead of feeling enriched. We do not finish what we start and ultimately our creativity dissipates because we do not consider it as important as some other aspects of our lives.

A great discipline to adopt is to ask yourself consistently why you do what you do. When you take on yet another task, why are you doing it? When you say you want to be involved in something, what is the real reason? I live by the saying that there are many GOOD things you can do, but only a few GODLY things to which you should devote your time.

When you scale down and focus, you will have more time to allow your creativity to flourish. You will also enjoy life a whole lot more. In fact, you will be more creative in everything you do, even the menial things.

An example in my own life is my song writing. If all I am doing is performing, touring, or ministering, even though I love doing this, and they are all important facets of what I do, I feel burnt out and restless. This is because I know that what fulfils me and keeps me "refuelled" is my writing. If I do not make regular time to do this, I begin to feel frustrated and dissatisfied.

When I find time to write every week, I feel energized to do everything else I need to do. It has taken me several years to realize that it centers me when I create space to write. Before I made time for this, I had so many distractions I was jumping from one thing to the next; so much was happening it was like spinning ten plates in the air, and I knew that sooner or later they were all going to come crashing down. Life is still busy, but I now try to focus my energies on what I know God has called me to do, and I always make sure I have time to write. I do not always get it right, but I'm much better than I used to be.

What is it that brings you peace? Is it painting, watching a movie, reading a book, worshipping to a CD at home? Discipline yourself to make time for these moments, and do not feel guilty about it. God made you unique and wants you to find ways that will expand the creative spirit within you.

Creating space

In her book *The Creative Call*,[18] Janice Elshiemer talks about the art of listening and how it creates space for her to hear and be inspired by God. I love this concept because it encourages us to stop, breathe and think, instead of rushing head-on into things. She believes that it puts us in a place of expectation so that we can hear what God wants to say.

She quotes the author Madeline L'Engle: "As I listen to the silence, I can learn that my feelings about art and my feelings about the creator of the universe are inseparable."

Listening is an art in itself. It is amazing how creating a space to listen helps generate ideas, and teaches us about God and the gift of creativity that He has placed in us.

Stop right now and listen to what is going on around you. Can you hear the wind, or the rain outside? Or maybe crickets or birds singing? Can you hear the tick of a clock, or the sound of the waves? Can you hear the rhythm of cars driving to and from their destination? Can you hear God trying to speak to you? What is He saying?

Setting time aside to work on your craft

Most creative people lack the ability to put structure in place. We are driven by moments of inspiration, and this means that setting aside a specific time during the week to work on our craft can be difficult, and dare I say it, boring. However, as I have expressed earlier, if we wait for moments of greatness, we could be waiting quite a while! Making time in your diary to be creative is vital for the process of creativity to take place. Space is just as important as inspiration.

If I do not make the time, most often creativity does not happen. Of course, there will be moments when I will have a flash of inspiration, and that is wonderful. This is preferable to trying to search for it, but it does not happen as much as I would like, so I need to discipline myself by setting aside some time. Alternatively, it's easy to receive a moment of inspiration and have no space to expand our ideas further.

Making time to work on your craft could be practicing your singing, going to arts school, writing a few chapters of your book, writing songs, sketching, painting, or undertaking a course in photography. It may simply mean going to the gym, taking a walk or going to a café on your own with a good book. All these things regenerate you, teach you and discipline you. (Ouch, there's that word again!)

The story of the disciples fishing all night is a wonderful example of discipline:

Luke 5:4–6 *When He finished teaching, He said to Simon, "Push out into deep water and let your nets out for a catch." Simon said, "Master, we've been fishing hard all night and haven't caught even a minnow. But if you say so, I'll let out the nets." It was no sooner said than done—a huge haul of fish, straining the nets past capacity.*[19]

Sometimes, when we are trying to be disciplined it can feel like we are "working all night" just like this scripture expresses.

However, there is the possibility that if the disciples had not worked hard all night, they would not have had the experience or the ability for the last haul. God uses all things as training for the time when you will need all the skills you have learned.

You were designed to move out into the deep waters, just like a boat. He is calling you to radical obedience. He is calling you to go deeper. He is probably asking you to do something you do not think you can do. Guess what? You can do it! You *will* succeed. And the blessings and fruit of that will eventually overtake your life.

For the disciples to catch the big haul, they had to sit still and throw their anchor overboard. We sometimes think that if we are not moving forward all the time then we must be failing. To rest and wait is a discipline in itself. Sometimes the season requires us to sit still as it is the only way to receive what lies deep in His waters. He wants us to be anchored in Him so that we will not just sail without purpose—we will have focus, steadfastness and the strength of Him being our anchor. As you can see, a life of discipline comes in many forms and has its own set of challenges, but it also has its rewards.

When the going gets tough and you are feeling as if you are getting nowhere, just keep going. Keep pushing forward;

you will eventually push through to the next level. I believe that you can do it!

Finish well

Finally, always determine to finish well.

> Ecc 7:8 **Endings are better than beginnings. Sticking to it is better than standing out.**[20]

Many people start something because they think it sounds like a great idea at the time. But it is rare that people finish things. Why? Because the thrill of something new will eventually wear off, and then all that is left is hard work. I commend people on our worship team who have been there for many years, because they have served faithfully in both exciting times, and during times of sheer hard work. One conference is a new experience, but after ten or more conferences, they are still excited and passionate about serving in the Kingdom. That is discipline and I am so proud of them.

I believe that anything that is worth something will cost you something. Sometimes the cost is big, sometimes the cost is small, but it will definitely cost you.

There is something that happens on the inside of us when we determine in our spirits to finish well, even when we do not feel like it. I remember sitting in a practice exam during my last year of High School and my self-talk was poor. I felt as if I was not smart enough to pass and because of fear of failure, I walked out without completing the exam. I figured it was easier to decide to fail than to give it a go and fail anyway! Then I began to imagine what my life would be like if I did not complete my last year of High School. I wondered if it would set a pattern for the rest of my life if I started things and never finished them. The thought scared me. I needed to go back and finish what I had started. After reasoning this (and receiving a stern chat from my parents), I went back and completed my exams. I was nervous, it was hard, and I was scared that I would fail, but I did it, and I passed with flying colors!

I learnt a big lesson that year, one that forever influenced my life. I was so encouraged that I was able to finish and finish well, that it has become an important aspect for me in trying to lead a successful life. I often wonder if I had not completed that last year how it would have affected other decisions that I've made over the years. Not just academically, but spiritually.

Finishing well is also important because if you do finish well, you will then start the next thing well. You create strong links in a chain that cannot be broken. If you build on good foundations, you will have a strong house.

In the tough times, I question myself if I find that I want to give up on something. If the reason is that it is too hard, then that is not a good enough reason to quit. If it is because I realize I'm not passionate about something, or it does not fit into the goals I want to achieve in my life, or I can't juggle it with everything else I'm doing, then I will lay it down. It is a wise person who knows when to quit. However, it is also a wise person who knows when to finish well.

I want to end this chapter by sharing a lovely story by Lewis Carroll that is recounted in Madeline L'Engle's book *Walking on Water*. It reflects on the importance of discipline as a daily act:

> *There's a story of a small village (about the size of the village near Crosswicks) where lived an old clockmaker and repairer. When anything was wrong with any of the clocks or watches in the village, he was able to fix them, to get them working properly again. When he died, leaving no children and no apprentice, there was no one left in the village who could fix clocks. Soon various clocks and watches began to break down.*

Those which continued to run often lost or gained time, so they were of little use. A clock might strike midnight at three in the afternoon. So many of the villages abandoned their timepieces.

One day a renowned clockmaker and repairer came through the village, and the people crowded around him and begged him to fix their broken clocks and watches. He spent many hours looking at all the faulty timepieces, and at last he announced that he could repair only those whose owners had kept them wound, because they were the only ones which would be able to remember how to keep time.

So, every day we must keep things wound. That is, we must pray when prayer seems as dry as dust; we must write when we are physically tired, when our hearts are heavy, when our bodies are in pain. We may not always be able to make our "clock" run correctly, but at least we can keep it wound so that it will not forget.[21]

The artist and forgiveness

Forgiveness is not just something we grant another person.
It is a gift we give ourselves.[22]
The Creative Call by Janice Elsheimer

A story that has been retold over the centuries concerns Michelangelo painting the ceiling of the Sistine Chapel. His father had come to speak with him and an argument ensued. When Michelangelo returned to paint, he could not paint the faces of his work because he was angry with his father. After a while, he reasoned that his anger was the cause of his inability to continue and so he returned to speak with his father. It was only after they had forgiven and embraced each other that Michelangelo was able to return to painting his historic work.

I love this story because it shows the power forgiveness can hold in a God artist's life. Deep-seated bitterness and the inability to forgive can prevent the greatest artist from ever reaching their true potential. You might assume that feelings such as these will not affect your creativity in any way, but eventually you will reach a point where you will suffer from the harmful effects that a lack of forgiveness can bring.

> Matt 6:14–15 *In prayer there is a connection between what God does and what you do. You can't get forgiveness from God, for instance, without also forgiving others. If you refuse to do your part, you cut yourself off from God's part.*[23]

This scripture is saying that if I do not forgive others, God cannot forgive me. This means I am cut off from all God has for me and am unable to tap into the source of the greatest creative power supply I could encounter. If I am removed from this power supply, then I am only creating from the resources that are inside of me—from the realms of my gift. When I create just from my gift, I create in my own strength, because I am not being energized by my relationship with God. I will continue to be creative, but if I want to create something that is bigger than me, I need to be connected to God. Yet if I do not forgive, I will not have that connection in the most powerful way possible. Eventually, if I am not filled by God's presence, I begin to create out of what I know and who I am.

Great people have created in this way and can continue to create for the rest of their lives, but imagine what they could have been if they tapped into the source! When something is great, but could be even greater, we are actually settling for second best, no matter how many accolades we receive from people who view our art.

In my own life I know the power that forgiveness has brought me. My scope for writing expanded greatly when I began the process of forgiving others and myself. I also found my relationship with the Lord deepened and became more transparent. I truly believe this type of change also makes your art deep and transparent. This is a process that evolves over a lifetime—forgiveness is not something that you deal with and afterwards everything is fine. There will be many situations in our lifetime that will challenge us to either forgive or take offence. The test for us is: which path will we choose?

You may feel that you do not have unforgiveness in your heart, or maybe you feel justified in harbouring resentment towards someone who has done something to you. I want to encourage you to search your heart for anything that could prevent you from fulfilling your potential, so let us explore this topic together and see what the Lord reveals to you. This is not meant to bring condemnation, but restoration and freedom.

Nancy Leigh Demoss, author of *Choosing Forgiveness*, says that in most of her seminars and conferences, close to 95 per cent of people admitted that at some time in their life they had not been able to forgive someone. These seminars often include leaders, long-time believers and vocational Christian workers. Her experience has led her to believe that most people have someone they need to forgive. This topic of forgiveness is not only vital to the artist, but to every member of the body of Christ.[24]

What is meant by unforgiveness or the feeling of bitterness?

The simplest explanation for unforgiveness is feeling hurt by someone's actions and/or words, and in turn letting that hurt linger without resolve. Someone once said, "Unforgiveness is like drinking poison and hoping someone else will die." That is an accurate description not only of what it can do to other people, but what it can do to you personally.

Unforgiveness often goes hand in hand with bitterness. The word for bitterness in the original Greek is "pik," which means to prick or cut. That is certainly how unforgiveness can feel at times. Have you ever had a paper cut on your hand? For something seemingly so small, it can cause quite a lot of pain. Anything that touches that cut will make it sting. It may not be clearly visible to you unless you look closely at it, yet it can be very uncomfortable. Unforgiveness is just like that—it cuts a small hole in your heart. People may not see it at first, but it will cause pain to the whole body.

Some other meanings for the word "forgive" in the Merriam Webster Online Dictionary are "to give up resentment of" and "to cease to feel resentment against (an offender)."[25] We can safely say that to be an unforgiving person means you hold resentment to someone who has caused offence to you.

How do I know if I have unforgiveness in my heart?

Unforgiveness can affect how you see certain situations that may seem similar to past hurts. You may want to withdraw just to protect yourself. There is nothing wrong in this, but it is a concern to the Lord when unforgiveness is long standing, is painful for you and transfers to many situations in your life.

Look at the list below and honestly ask yourself if you have experienced any of these feelings towards another person. If you have, then you are most probably harbouring bitterness, resentment, and ultimately unforgiveness:[26]

- You replay an incident concerning the other person repeatedly in your mind.
- When you think about a person or incident, uncomfortable feelings surface such as anger, hurt or resentment.
- You are so hurt that you try to avoid the person or situation, and try not to think about them at all by blocking them completely out of your life and your thoughts.
- Even though you may be a genuinely nice person, you secretly hope something bad happens to the other person to teach them a lesson.

- You tell others repeatedly how a person or situation has hurt you and you talk about it often.
- If other people speak about this person, you feel uncomfortable, or speak badly about them.
- You always avoid a person who has hurt you.

Why is forgiveness so important to me as a worshipper and God artist?

There are several reasons why forgiveness affects how you worship God, and also how it influences your creativity.

Bitterness affects our whole lives—*not just one part of it.* It is like a pure drink of water: if we put just one spoonful of vinegar or salt in it, it will affect the taste. Unforgiveness may seem small and insignificant in terms of the rest of our lives, but it will inevitably permeate everything we do, say and feel. The sad thing is, we won't even realize it because we can become used to the taste of vinegar after a while!

> Heb 12:15 *Keep a sharp eye out for weeds of bitter discontent. A thistle or two gone to seed can ruin a whole garden in no time.*[27]

The story of Judah (Genesis 38), one of Joseph's brothers, is an example of bitterness that was harboured for almost a whole lifetime. After he allowed Joseph to be sold into slavery, trouble followed him. His two sons died of unexplainable causes, his wife died, and he became a bitter and tormented man. Imagine the relief he must have felt when Joseph, despite all the sins committed against him by his brothers, forgave them and welcomed them into his household. And even though forgiveness can be hard to offer at times, imagine the power of release that Joseph would have experienced. He had not seen his brothers for many years, and he was able to forgive them for what they had done to him in the past.

It is impossible to be a bitter person and to have an intimate relationship with God. Do you know what happens? Instead of having a relationship you become religious. What's wrong with that? Well, faith becomes about following the rules and doing the right thing rather than having a personal connection with God. Your unforgiveness, bitterness or resentment will affect how you relate to God. If you are someone who wants to minister to people through your art, yet you are not able to connect with God, your bitterness will be the ruling factor in all you do.

Bitterness can affect your creativity. Bitterness can makes you critical. It can cause blockages. Forgiveness and progressive creativity cannot reside together in harmony because they go against each other.

Bitterness affects your health. Bitterness has been linked to physiological and physical ill-health. High blood pressure, a low immune system, memory loss and hormonal dysfunction are all common complaints of those who carry bitterness in their heart.

Bitterness affects our relationship with God and others. Most people who are bitter find it difficult to accept God's love and forgiveness for their own lives. If we do not forgive others, we will find it hard to receive forgiveness for ourselves.

> Galatians 6:7 *Do not be deceived: God cannot be mocked. A man reaps what he sows.*[28]

If we truly live by the thought that we reap what we sow, then how we treat others is how we will be treated. Our relationship with others and with God is affected.

Bitterness allows the enemy a door into our lives.

> Ephesians 4:26–27 *In your anger do not sin: Do not let the sun go down while you are still angry, and do not give the devil a foothold.*[29]

All the enemy needs to work against you is one small foothold and he can hold you back from achieving your full potential. Unforgiveness is often hidden below the surface, but it is one of the greatest tactics of the devil in preventing you from fulfilling your calling truthfully and completely. In terms of being an artist, you can write or paint and it will bless many people, but have you ever felt that there was something missing? That there was a greater measure of your calling yet to be fulfilled? Is it possible that unforgiveness has been holding you back all these years? This is not always the case, but it is definitely a point to look at, and one that should not be overlooked when you are evaluating your life.

Is there any sin that cannot be forgiven?

Throughout scripture, there is only one sin that is considered to be unforgivable, and it is found in:

> Mark 3:29 *But whoever blasphemes against the Holy Spirit will never be forgiven; he is guilty of an eternal sin.*
> (Other references include Matt 12:31–32, and Luke 12:10).[30]

To put it simply, to blaspheme against the Holy Spirit means that a person would reject the convicting influence of God and His salvation. If someone turns away from Christ knowing that the Son of God died for our sins, that would be an unforgivable sin.

Many people have been concerned that they may have committed the unforgivable sin. Do not feel condemned if you have found yourself in this position. The fact that you would be concerned shows a heart of repentance towards the Lord. Our God is so gracious and there have been many who have rejected Him, yet at a crucial point in their lives, or even on their deathbed, they have repented and have asked Him into their hearts. It is never too late to ask for Christ's forgiveness.

God is a God of forgiveness

Micah 7:19 *And compassion is on its way to us. You'll stamp out our wrongdoing. You'll sink our sins to the bottom of the ocean.*[31]

The prophet Micah is saying here that all our sins are thrown into the deepest part of the sea, giving the impression that they are taken far away from us—somewhere deep and unfathomable so that they can never be found. That sounds to me as if God is interested in forgiving! Of course, sin has repercussions. Murder is punishable by death or jail, even though God is willing to forgive the repentant heart.

1 Peter 3:18 *For Christ died for sins once for all, the righteous for the unrighteous, to bring you to God.*[32]

Christ died for all sins. That is everything. We forgive and love with our hearts, but we must also live with wisdom, boundaries and truth. Forgiveness does not mean you allow people to hurt you repeatedly; however, it does mean you let them go—you release them into the hands of God.

Let me point out here that you may not always see the results of forgiveness. People may still act towards you in the same way. Some people may not accept your forgiveness, or they may choose not to forgive you, even when you are repentant. Rest in the confidence that God sees your heart and that is whose opinion really matters.

How can I tell if I have truly forgiven?

Sometimes it is hard to know if you have truly forgiven. The book *Choosing Forgiveness* shares some signposts that indicate that you are on the path to forgiveness:

- You want the best for the other person.
- You rejoice when you hear they have done well.

- You have identified that you have unforgiveness or bitterness in your heart, and you have prayed to God and asked for forgiveness for harbouring this resentment, and in doing so, have released them into His hands.
- You take responsibility for your part of the equation. If that means all you need to do is to release the hurt and forgive them, then that is all that needs to happen. You do not always need to speak with the person who has hurt you. Remember, forgiveness is about what is happening in your heart.

However, if you have been the cause of some pain, you may need to set your pride aside and ask for forgiveness. This may mean saying sorry and approaching the person whom you have hurt (but this is not always the case—every situation is different). This is not easy and it is uncomfortable. Nevertheless, God encourages the process of restoration! It is so important to the Father to see his flock loving each other and working together, even when it is difficult for them to do so.

Have you been Christlike? Forgiveness is not a feeling; it is an act of your will.

Understand that this process is going to feel uncomfortable. It's so powerful when we try to protect unity at all costs, especially when we desire to establish and maintain friendships.

Psalm 133:1 *How good and pleasant it is when brothers live together in unity!*[33]

Can I forgive?

It is possible to forgive even the greatest wrong done to you. It is possible to forgive yourself. If it were not so, the Lord would not encourage you to be a forgiving person. It is because of His grace that we can forgive. Because of what He has done for us, forgiving mankind of sin and embracing us as sons, daughters and friends, we can forgive. It does not matter how big or difficult your situation is; God is bigger! He will walk this journey with you if you let him.

However, it is not possible to forgive like this on your own. You need God to show you how to love and forgive because it really is a supernatural act. I think that even those who do not know God, who choose to forgive horrendous crimes carried out against them, are walking in that supernatural power. It releases such power and healing that it is almost not of this world. God is working in their lives and they may not even realize it!

Nancy Leigh Jones says, "Forgiveness is not something you can give yourself—it is something he has purchased for you." This act of forgiveness is a gift from God.

For you to rise up above your hurt you need a revelation of how Christ died for you and has forgiven your sins. This is the foundation of your ability to forgive others. When we love and forgive like this, a great power is released supernaturally. A greater power than the sin itself.

Some practical exercises on forgiveness

If you find it a struggle, or painful to motivate yourself to forgive, here are some suggestions that may help you move forward on the journey of healing.

Write a letter

Write a letter to a person who has really discouraged you—but do not send it! Explain why they hurt you, but then tell them you forgive them and that you are free of resentment. When you have finished your letter, burn it and let God know you have let it go. (Let me stress again, do not send it!) Pray. Be honest with your feelings and make a decision to release that person and release forgiveness into your life.

Talk it out

Share your feelings with someone whom you can trust. Ask them to pray with you and keep you accountable. Give them permission to ask you how you are going on a regular basis.

Prayer of forgiveness

Pray a prayer of forgiveness. Here is an example below:

Dear Lord, I have been hurting inside, and I want to share those feelings with You now.

I realize that to have unforgiveness in my life causes me pain, and keeps me from moving forward in my life and it keeps me from drawing closer to You. God, I ask You to forgive me for holding unforgiveness. I do not want anything to come between my relationship with You.

Father, I want to confess right now that I forgive the people who have wronged me or hurt me in any way. I forgive

---

Lord, bless them. I pray they will come to know You in a power-ful way and that they would be changed by Your presence. I release them into Your hands. I pray for their every success and rejoice when they do well.

I thank You Lord that You also forgive me for my wrongdoing. I know that there is no condemnation in Christ Jesus and therefore do not need to harbour feelings of low self-worth and guilt. I am free because You made me free through Your blood on the cross. Continue to teach me to walk in Your ways, to love as You love, to forgive as You forgive.

From this moment forward, I confess that I am free from the resentment, bitterness and discouragement that my unforgive-ness has caused. I am a person full of hope, confidence, peace, faith and unity.

In Jesus name I pray, AMEN.

In conclusion, I want to rejoice with you that God will always use everything—even our painful experiences—for his glory. It is wonderful to know that just as you learn to forgive, you will be a great example for other people in learning how to forgive. Your experiences can become a tool to minister to others who are going through similar hurts.

> Revelation 12:11 *They overcame him (Satan) by the blood of the lamb, the word of their testimony, and they loved not their lives to the death.*

You have been forgiven through the blood of Jesus on the cross; your testimony is a testimony that can embrace the theme of forgiveness. This overcomes the evil one!

5

Artists as prophets

Straightaway the ideas flow in upon me, directly from God.[34]

Johannes Brahms

*H*ave you ever imagined creating something that was so powerful that it's effect was felt by nations around the world? Something from the work of your own hands that was relevant both culturally and politically?

Imagine completing a painting that captures the spirit of the people of New York after the 9/11 attacks. Not just any ordinary painting, but one that reflects the people's emotions, and the ash, sweat and tears as we see workers rebuilding the ruins of the twin towers. A painting that shows faith and hope for the future and pours strength into the hearts of all who look upon it. It would certainly capture the attention of the world, wouldn't it?

More than ever before it has become important for those of

us who are instilled with creative gifts to use them to their greatest measure possible. To dig deep, search far, reach as high as we can, sacrifice what we must, to create art that not only lasts, but relates the oracles of God to people who have never heard his voice. This is what you were called for. It is one of the highest callings on earth, and one that we must not take lightly. Search for it with all your heart, and do not settle for anything less.

The power of the prophetic

What I am talking about is for people to become prophetic worshippers. Today, they need to hear the voice of God for the moment, for their situation. A voice that relates instantly. Art is one of the greatest mediums for this because we are all captured by its beauty. When people are captivated by what they see and feel, they will be softened to hear the voice of the Spirit in a greater measure. Your work of art becomes a work of worship.

It is possible to create like this. Sculptures by Michelangelo, such as those of David, or of Mary holding her dead son Jesus (the "Pieta"), have created a lasting impact over centuries, and they still affect millions of people today. Even though Michelangelo was known to be an arrogant and eccentric man, he had a gift for capturing emotions in his art. He was able to sculpt events and people from earlier times, and in doing so, he recreated a moment that put in motion the truth of the Bible for all to see and experience. This was a prophetic act, one that he may not have realized himself, but one that has stood the test of time.

You may have heard of Akiane, the brilliant child poet and painter. At the age of four, she was already drawing pictures that many adults could not even attempt to paint. Some of her most famous works include her captivating picture of Jesus called *Prince of Peace*. Her collection includes paintings of Heaven (from visions she has encountered), Jesus praying as a boy, Jesus as a teenager, plus many stunning settings of nature and creation.

At the age of 12, she is already creating works that will last through the generations. However, she is not just an amazing talent. The prophetic is found in her paintings and poetry.

Akiane painted a work called *Found* when she was nine years old. It depicts two black infants in front of a waterfall in a jungle. One child appears to be aged between three and four months, and is lying on its stomach, while the other, aged between two and three years, gently and protectively has its hand on the other child's head. Here is what Akiane says about this painting:

> *I was inspired to paint all the races, but to find coloured people where I lived was very hard. After a lot of prayer, I met two black children whose story was so amazing that I wanted to paint it right away. There was a taboo in their small Madagascar tribe against saving the orphans. So, after their parents died, the two-year-old brother was taking care of his three-month-old sister for over two months. When they were found, they were barely alive. I painted them older and healthier to create what their vision might have been during the three-month survival. The baby girl has noticed the help approaching and is gently caressing her exhausted brother to lift his head up.*
>
> *After I invited the adoptive parents to look at the finished portrait, they were crying. Although I had painted five different backgrounds complete with deserts, animals, birds and prairies I decided to paint the waterfalls at the very end. Everybody including me was surprised at the painted waterfalls in the background, because I had not known that the orphans had been found in the only water-fall jungle in the Madagascar.*[35]

Akiane did more than paint a beautiful picture. She prophetically sensed their past and declared a future of hope. Not only did she paint a waterfall, not knowing that this was the place where the children were found, but she painted the children to look older and stronger. This is an encouraging word from the Lord for her adoptive parents. I believe God was reaffirming to those who care for these children that they would be safe and that they would grow up to be strong.

I want to be the kind of God artist that influences people with the presence of God. It is a huge honour to be chosen in such a time as this, and we must do all we can to bring God's word to a lost generation that needs redemption. Your art could be the only godly work they ever see or hear, so paint well, write well, dance well, sing well, do what you must in freedom and strength to be the kind of artist who encapsulates the prophetic.

Perhaps this is an overwhelming thought for you. I want to inspire you as you read this to know that God has given you a gift and when you go deeper with Him, He will draw it out of you. Please do not think you cannot be this type of artist, because you can! If He created you, He is big enough to create in you as well.

The journey of life will mean that we will all be searching for creative expression during our lives and learning more as we create. However, there are some foundations upon which we can build. As you read on, I pray that God will speak to you about what steps you need to take in your heart and in your mind to pave the way.

Understanding the prophetic

Firstly, it is important to understand what it means to be prophetic. Most people would rightly assume that to be a prophet means to foretell the future. But that is not all a prophet does. In ancient times, prophets were also called "seers." Their primary role was not to foretell the future, but rather to pray humbly and earnestly to God, and to preach of the righteousness of God to the people.

The word "seer" in ancient Hebrew (ra'ah) means a "seeing person"—one who "perceives mentally the purpose of God."[36] Prophets were also called "Chozeh," which means "a beholder; one who has visions or supernatural revelations."

Dake's annotated reference Bible says this about prophets: *A prophet ... always had extraordinary commission, receiving their messages by direct inspiration and being moved upon and carried along by the Holy Spirit as a leaf is carried along with a strong wind.*[37]

To be prophetic means to use our gifts to create art that speaks on behalf of God. Just like the prophet, you have an extraordinary commission and you can receive inspiration from God. This may not always happen, but like a leaf carried by the wind, the Holy Spirit will carry us and place us where we need to be.

You are someone who mentally perceives the purposes of God. This means that you can put into pictures what God is trying to say. You can capture His heart and place it in a form that will reach people. I always pray that when I write a song I am able to capture what the Lord wants. I may not always do this, but I spend my life in pursuit of knowing Him well enough to be able to place who He is in what I do.

When you create prophetically, you create with insight. You can delve into the core of what needs to be said, and you can be confident that you are declaring a truth that will radically change people's lives. You become more than an artist; you become a social reformer, a teacher, a preacher, a worshipper!

How do we become prophetic?

When we accept Jesus as Lord and saviour into our lives, we have the prophetic in us. Some people have the gift of being true prophets in the sense of being able to foretell the future, and knowing specific details and events of people's lives (there is a difference between being prophetic, and having the role of being a prophet—in this chapter we are primarily focusing on being prophetic). But all of God's people have the inner spirit of prophecy in terms of the description we have discussed above.

Rev 10:19b **Worship God. For the testimony of Jesus is the spirit of prophecy.**[38]

Do you have a testimony? If you have been saved and have accepted Jesus into your heart and life, you do have it. That means that if you worship him, you will have the spirit of prophecy. We reveal who Jesus is when we worship him. And this testimony of who Jesus is, is the spirit of prophecy! To put it simply, if you want to become more prophetic, worship him more.

Pablo Perez in his book *The Prophetic Worshipper* gives this profound testimony:

> *More than a decade ago, I was part of a worship team. I played the piano in services and sang on occasion. I realized that my music did not have life. It was only an expression of technique, hollow and empty.*
>
> *I couldn't stand this situation any longer, so I went to a man of God and said, "I feel empty and dry. My music does not transmit life, only death. I can't stand being like this any more and do not want to play just to play, and sing just to sing. I desire the Holy Spirit to flow through me. What should I do so that the life of God floods my being and is reflected in my music?"*
>
> *I have never forgotten the answer that this man gave me. He said, "The only way to transmit life is to find it. You have to have a personal and true encounter with Jesus because He is the life. Then, in the measure that you abide in Him and develop an intimate relationship with God, your music will reflect His life, and it won't be empty and dead any more."*
>
> *I was worried about the music but needed God in my whole being, I couldn't separate one from the other. If there*

was going to be life in the music, it would be because life was
coming from the depth of my heart.[39]

Friends, this may be the simplest truth, but it is a profound truth. For too long we have worshipped worship, or worshipped our art. We spend so much time thinking about what we create that we forget about the creator. If we spend time in God's arms, we will know Him and that will permeate our lives. We cannot separate the degree to which we know Him from our art. It will affect how we create. The more we know Him, the more scope we have in every area of our lives for growth and success.

Knowing Him changes *things*. But knowing him intimately changes *everything*.

Workshop ideas

If you feel you are stagnating creatively, the best thing you can do is to spend time with Him. Maybe you have not done this before. If you are not used to doing this, here are some practical suggestions for you:

1. Find a chapter in the Psalms that accurately reflects how you are feeling about whom God is. If you play an instrument, sit down in a quiet place and begin to sing out the Psalm. Even though I have written many songs this way, the intention is not to write a song, it is to express in our heart who God is. Play and sing whatever comes into your mind. Do not think too hard. Do not worry if it does not make sense—this is meant to be a learning experience. If you do not play an instrument, just sing your heart out! If you can't sing, wear earplugs! Just rejoice in God and enjoy expressing this in a different way.

2. Go for a walk. Take in all your surroundings. What do you hear? What do you see? Talk to God about what you

see and hear. Ask him to speak to you, and create the space to allow this to happen.

3. Keep a dream journal. You will be amazed at how much the Lord is actually trying to get your attention. Dreams are one of God's primary ways in which He speaks to me. (My friends say this is because He can't get a word in during the day!) Write down your dreams even if they do not make sense. You will eventually get into the habit of knowing when God is trying to speak to you or when the pizza you ate the night before is trying to speak to you. Read back over your dream journal entry and ask the Lord what He is trying to say to you. There are also some great book recommendations on understanding your dreams at the end of this chapter.[40]

4. Create space for silence. We do not have enough silence in our lives. There are so many voices, so many opinions, that it can be difficult to connect with God. Instead of leaving the TV on, turn it off. Turn your mobile phone off for an hour. I find that even if I clean the house with no other distractions, the space allows God room to speak.

5. When you are ministering to others, whether on a platform or person to person in your relationships, ask God to speak to you about the people to whom you are ministering. Ask him to show you one thing you could say, do, write, paint, sing, etc., that could impact upon them. Focus your attention on what you believe God wants for their lives. You will be amazed and encouraged to know that the Lord will use moments like this to give you creative ideas to bless others.

Matt Redman, worship leader, songwriter and author, says: "There's a sense in which the prophetic flows from that place of intimacy. You have to be close to God to hear His voice . . .

He speaks with a whisper. He maybe shouts to His enemies but to His friends He whispers. If you want to sing, play or dance prophetically, it has to come out of a place which is close to God . . . where you hear His voice, you become His spokesperson."[41]

Prophetic worship is powerful

Prophetic worship can declare the greatness of God when under attack, and change the spiritual atmosphere

Prophetic worship was, and still is, powerful. When King Jehoshaphat discovered that Judah was about to be invaded by Moab, Ammon and Edom, he enquired of the Lord. Through a prophet, Jahaziel, the Lord tells Jehoshaphat that the battle belonged to Him. Instead of sending his best soldiers to lead the front line, he had the singers and musicians go first, prophetically declaring the victory of the Lord.

> 2 Chronicles 21–22 **After consulting the people, Jehoshaphat appointed men to the Lord and to praise Him for the splendor of His holiness as they went out at the head of the army saying: "Give thanks to the Lord, for His love endures forever." As they began to sing and praise, the Lord set ambushes against the men of Ammon and Moah and Mount Seir who were invading Judah, and they were defeated.**[42]

Can you imagine how powerful this act would have been as they went out to fight? Hearing the hope of God in their ears rather than the sound of battle as they warred against their enemies. And quite daunting for the enemy too!

Prophetic worship can bring the peace of God and demons will have to flee

Prophetic worship can soothe the soul and bring peace. When Saul was tormented by an evil spirit, he would have David play music to him and the evil spirit would depart.

1 Samuel 16:22 *Whenever the spirit from God came upon Saul, David would take his harp and play. Then relief would come to Saul; he would feel better, and the evil spirit would leave him.*[43]

It is no wonder that King David commanded that there be twenty-four hour worship in the tabernacle. He understood the power of declaring the greatness of God.

Wouldn't you love your worship of God to soothe the spirit of those who are tormented? Imagine for a moment how your art could be so powerful that it could push back the enemy's plans, and that it could be an instrument of war in the supernatural that fights against evil and brings sweet victory.

Characteristics of a prophet

The office of a prophet and the gift of prophecy can be two different things. Even though a prophet can prophesy, people can have the gift of prophecy and not operate in the office of a prophet. We are not going to study the office of a prophet here, but as we have previously mentioned, all of us can have the *spirit* of prophecy regardless of what our predominant spiritual giftings are. It is a gift for everyone, because:

Rev 10:19 *. . . the testimony of Jesus is the spirit of prophecy.*[44]

The best way to create space for the prophetic is to study examples from the Bible. Below is a brief study on the characteristics of a prophet in biblical times. As you study them, ask the Lord to show you how you can apply these principles and translate them into your life as a God artist.

A prophet only spoke what God wanted them to speak, not what others wanted them to speak

Micaiah the prophet was such a man. In 1 Kings 22, Jehoshaphat, the King of Judah asks Ahab the King of Israel if there are any prophets they can consult before the battle with the King of Aram. Ahab brings in false prophets, around four hundred men, who all tell him that he should go to war because he will have victory.

Jehoshaphat asks again:

> (vs7) *Is there not a prophet of the Lord here whom we can inquire of?*[45]

The King of Judah said that there was such a prophet, but he does not like him because he never says anything good about Him (there's a clue right there!).

This is where Micaiah enters the story. A messenger is sent to Micaiah. The messenger says to him (paraphrased), *Micaiah, every other prophet has said that we should fight the King of Aram, so why don't you say the same thing? Be nice and just confirm what all the other prophets are saying. After all, 400 prophets can't be wrong!* Micaiah says to the messenger: *As surely as the Lord lives, I can only tell him only what the Lord tells me.* He was not intimidated. He knew he could only speak what God spoke.

This is where the story becomes interesting. Micaiah is brought before the Kings, as the four hundred false prophets continue to prophesy over them (no doubt this was an intimidating experience). Micaiah initially says exactly the same thing as the other prophets: *Go and fight, for you will be victorious.* Ahab realizes that something is wrong, because Micaiah always prophesied against him. When he enquires of Micaiah again, he finds out the truth: not only would they be defeated, but Ahab would be killed in this battle. In front of two Kings and four hundred other prophets, he unashamedly spoke what the Lord revealed, taking no account for the value of his own life. This was a man whom the Lord knew He could trust to speak His truth, regardless of the consequences.

Pablo Perez says: "We should be transmitters of the signal of Heaven, not just 'echoes' of what we hear other men say."[46]

To be prophetic means we do not just repeat what we have heard, it means we repeat what God puts in our hearts. Sometimes that may mean we are going against the crowd. If you have a word burning in your heart, do not be afraid to give it expression through your art, even if it means that it is completely different from what other people are presenting. If it is in line with the scriptures, then be confident that what you are speaking will bring life. After all, it's the word of God that lasts, and the word of God that changes lives.

They communicated the secret things of God

God shared his heart with His prophets, because He knew He could trust them.

> Amos 3:7 **Surely the Sovereign Lord does nothing without revealing His plan to His servants the prophets.**[47]

They were bold and undaunted

Undaunted means to be courageously resolute, especially in the face of danger or difficulty. They were not easily discouraged.

> Ezekiel 2:6 **And you, son of man, do not be afraid of them or their words. Do not be afraid, though briers and thorns are all around you and you live among scorpions. Do not be afraid of what they say or terrified by them, though they are a rebellious house.**[48]

They were alert, watchful and faithful

They needed to be vigilant. They were the watchmen and they kept their eyes open. They were on guard in case of attack or evil. In a sense, they were gatekeepers for their people.

> Ezekiel 3:17 **Son of man, I have made you a watchman for the house of Israel; so hear the word I speak and give them warning from Me.**[49]

They were attentive to God's voice

Ezekiel 3:10 *And He said to me, "Son of man, listen carefully and take to heart all the words I speak to you."* [50]

They sometimes uttered their predictions in verse, or music

Deuteronomy 32:44 *Moses came with Joshua son of Nun and spoke all the words of this song in the hearing of the people.* [51]

1 Samuel 10:5 *After that you will go to Gibeah of God, where there is a Philistine outpost. As you approach the town, you will meet a procession of prophets coming down from the high place with lyres, tambourines, flutes and harps being played before them, and they will be prophesying.* [52]

2 Kings 3:15 *But now bring me a harpist. While the harpist was playing, the hand of the Lord came upon Elisha . . .* [53]

They were committed to writing God's word down to have a record

Jeremiah 36:2 *Take a scroll and write on it all the words I have spoken to you concerning Israel, Judah and all the other nations from the time I began speaking to you in the reign of Josiah till now.* [54]

They were led by the Holy Spirit

2 Peter 1:21 *For prophecy never had its origin in the will of man, but men spoke from God as they were carried along by the Holy Spirit.* [55]

They were often given great power by God

There are many examples of how the prophets were endowed

with the power of God and the supernatural occurred. Here is one example of Moses:

> Exodus 4:1–4 *Moses answered, "What if they do not believe me or listen to me and say, 'The Lord did not appear to you.'?"*
>
> *Then the Lord said to him, "What is that in your hand?" "A staff," he replied.*
>
> *The Lord said, "Throw it on the ground." Moses threw it on the ground and it became a snake, and he ran from it.*
>
> *Then the Lord said to him, "Reach out your hand and take it by the tail." So Moses reached out and took hold of the snake and it turned back into a staff in his hand.*[56]

They could interpret dreams

> Daniel 1:17 *To these four young men God gave knowledge and understanding of all kinds of literature and learning. And Daniel could understand visions and dreams of all kinds.*[57]

They were humble

Although the prophets were strong and courageous, they were also humble, which is why the Lord was able to use them.

> Is 57:14–15 *For thus says the high and lofty one who inhabits eternity, whose name is Holy: "I dwell in the high and holy place, with him who has a contrite and humble spirit, to revive the spirit of the humble, and to revive the heart of the contrite ones."*[58]

How God "downloaded" information to the prophets

God can speak in various ways to his people. Here are some examples of how you can expect to hear his voice. If you are open and aware, you will find that the Lord is speaking more than you realize.

By dreams and visions

> Numbers 12:6 **Listen to My words: When a prophet of the Lord is among you, I reveal myself to him in visions, I speak to him in dreams.**[59]

In an audible voice

> 1 Sam 3:10 **The Lord came and stood there, calling as at the other times, "Samuel! Samuel!" Then Samuel said, "Speak, for Your servant is listening."**[60]

At schools or in training

In 2 Kings 3:5 there are references to the "company of prophets." In 1 Sam 19:20, Samuel was a leader of a group of prophets who were prophesying together. So, even though they were gifted by God, they still needed to learn from other prophets who were wise and more experienced.

By angels

> Revelation 22:8–9 **I, John, am the one who heard and saw these things. And when I had heard and seen them, I fell down to worship at the feet of the angel who had been showing them to me.**
>
> **But he said to me, Do not do it! I am a fellow servant with you and with your brothers the prophets and of all who keep the words of this book. Worship God!**[61]

Conclusion

When you write a song, a story, a dance or a play, are you creating what you believe the Lord wants you to create, or what you think will be most accepted? What is more important? When you paint, perform, lead worship or play music, do you translate His heart with boldness, without feeling discouraged? Are you alert and watchful for His creative words to come, ready at any time to receive them and faithful enough to deliver them? Are you attentive to receive all He has to say, or do you fight it to do what you want? Are you willing to learn, study and train to become more prophetic in your art under the authority of scripture?

God is looking for people who want to be led by the Holy Spirit to create art that speaks of Him. He searches the face of the Earth looking for the God artist whom he can empower with his supernatural presence. When you embrace the prophetic in your life, expect dreams, visions and encounters with angels. Once you have tasted this kind of life, you will never be satisfied unless you are creating with the power of God in you and working through you.

The artist and the tabernacle— our role as priests

But you are a chosen people, a royal priesthood, a holy nation, a people belonging to God, that you may declare the praises of Him who called you out of darkness into His wonderful light.[62]
1 Peter 2:9

You have made them to be a kingdom and priests to serve our God and they will reign on the earth.[63] Rev 5:10

*O*ver time, we have lost the value of what the Bible means when it talks about being "kings and priests." We live in an age where these roles are not represented fully in western culture. Yet the scriptures place enough importance on them for us to take notice and see how we can apply these ancient roles to our modern-day lives.

Many of the powerful awakenings of the church can be traced back to men and women fulfilling their roles as royal kings and priests. Evan Roberts and the 1904 Welsh revival is an example. Passionate prayer became primary in influencing the nation; it was not uncommon to hear and see Evan calling out to the Lord with a fervency that was contagious. The results were so influential that shopkeepers shortened their opening hours so that people could leave work in time to prepare for the nightly meetings. Prostitutes gave their hearts to the Lord and began to run their own Bible studies. Major sporting events were post-poned because people were more interested in attending the meetings! Like the priests of the Old Testament who brought requests in prayer to God, Evan Roberts led the way in standing in the gap for Wales.[64]

Prayer and worship played an integral role in the lives of priests in the tabernacle. Similarly, the King who worshipped and honoured God expanded his authority, influence and dominion. King David is an example of this. Having a greater understand-ing of these roles can help us to fulfil our own artistic callings to greater measure. How do we worship like priests? What kind of worship is pleasing to God? What is the connection between being a priest, and being a God artist?

To understand this, let's do a brief study of the tabernacles mentioned in the Old Testament. There are many books that study this in depth and I will only touch on some of the thoughts that I find relevant for us. For more information, please read the books mentioned in the Bibliography.

The tabernacles of Moses and David

There are three tabernacles mentioned in the Old Testament—the tabernacle of Moses and the tabernacle of David, which eventu-ally became known as Solomon's Temple.

The tabernacle was the place where God's glory dwelled. One word for Tabernacle in Hebrew is "ohel," which is translated to mean many words, one of which is "dwell" meaning "God dwells." It was the place where God's spirit abided, where He spoke and met with His people.

Let's study the furniture of the tabernacle and its significance. We will then study the role of the priest.

The curtains

The tabernacle consisted of two tents. The outer tent included the inner tent, but also had the outer courts, where the brazen alter and the brazen laver were kept (we will explain what these are a little later on). The inner tent was considered the inner tabernacle, the holy place, and the most holy place, where the Ark of the Covenant resided.

When the people entered the first tent, they did so through a veil, or curtain, made of fine twisted white linen interwoven with colors. These colors were blue, purple and scarlet. These colors represented different facets of God. Blue represented the heavens, or Lordship of God. Purple represented royalty. Scarlet represented the blood of the sacrifices brought to God by his people but also prophetically the blood of Christ which brought us salvation. These curtains were held up by gold hooks and pillars, which represented value.

The brazen altar

Through the curtains was the outer court of the tabernacle. Anyone could enter this part of the tabernacle, as long as they understood and respected that it was holy ground.

The first piece of furniture in the tabernacle was the brazen altar. This was where the priests would sacrifice animals as an offering to God. It was made of wood and was covered with copper.

This altar represented sacrifice. The sacrifice that Christ made by dying on the cross for us, and also the sacrifice of dying to ourselves—our wants and needs to serve the wants and needs of the King of Kings.

The brazen laver

After the brazen altar and before entering the next tent that was the door to the holy place, was the brazen laver. This was made of polished copper, and held water. The best way to describe it is that it looked like a huge birdbath filled with water. This was where the priests would wash themselves after giving sacrifices and before entering the holy place.

The second curtain

Once past the brazen laver, the priests would enter a second veil to enter the second tent. This second veil was the same as the first veil in terms of its colors—blue, purple and scarlet. After sacrifice, it was another reminder of the salvation, sovereignty and royalty of God.

Today, when we sacrifice something in our lives and then experience the pain of being "cleaned up" afterwards, it would be easy for us to forget the salvation and royalty of God. It is almost as if this second curtain reminds us to think on the greatness of God, rather than the pain of the sacrifice. It centers us again, and helps us to progress further in our journey with God, rather than allowing us to become caught up in works. It takes the focus off us and our pain and puts it back into the right perspective of a wonderful, sovereign God who has saved us from eternal death.

Inside this tent, there was the golden lamp stand, or candlestick, the table of shewbread and then the altar of incense in the holy place, and the Ark of the Covenant in what was called the most holy place.

The candlestick

The candlestick was housed on the left-hand side of this tent. It was made of pure gold, had seven branches, and burned olive oil for light. It was required to be lit at all times as the lamp stand was the only source of light in the tabernacle. The light from this candlestick represented the Holy Spirit.

The table of shewbread

On the right-hand side of the tent was the table of shewbread. This was a wooden table that was overlaid with gold. It held 12 cakes of unleavened bread, which symbolized the 12 tribes of Israel. They were positioned in two rows to signify unity, and then frankincense was placed on the top of each of these piles.

On the table of shewbread there was also wine that the priests poured as an offering. This signified prophecy and communion. The loaves, set in two rows, also represented this communion (as well as unity). They were continually bathed in the light of the Holy Spirit, represented by the lamp stand. It is interesting to note that without the Holy Spirit (the light of the candlestick), it is hard to see unity, or to have communion or fellowship (the loaves of shewbread and the wine). We need the Holy Spirit to help us to be a body of unity and communion; we cannot do it by our own strength alone.

The altar of incense

As the priest moved forward into the holy place, there was the altar of incense. This altar was lit by the fire that came from the brazen altar. The priest would then crumble incense upon it, and the fragrance would permeate right through to the Holy of Holies, which was where the Ark of the Covenant was held.

The altar of incense represented prayer and intercession. As this altar was lit from the fire from the brazen altar, it reminds us that for our prayers to be "lit" it will take sacrifice. It really does take sacrifice to pray.

The third curtain

After the altar of incense and before the Ark was the third curtain or the "veil." It was also made up of the three colors—blue, purple and scarlet. Again, a reminder of our sovereign God.

The Ark

In the Holy of Holies, there was only one piece of furniture, the Ark of the Covenant. This was a rectangular box that was overlaid with gold and had a lid of pure gold. This lid had two angels or cherubs rising up from it and was called "the mercy seat."

Inside the Ark was held a golden pot of manna, Aaron's rod that budded, and the Ten Commandments originally given to Moses by God on two tablets (the tablets of the law).[65]

The only light in the most holy place was a supernatural light that permeated from the mercy seat. This was the place where God spoke. It was truly a most holy place where only the high priests could come and give their offerings, minister, and speak with God.

The three elements that were in the Ark—the pot of manna, Aaron's rod that budded, and the law, also have great significance. The manna was a reminder of how God provided heavenly food for the Israelites as they were being led through the desert. Aaron's rod that budded was a reminder that God will choose whom He chooses, not man—and that it was not open to debate (Numbers 17). The tablets of the law were to remind people of how God wanted them to live. It was a reminder of who God was and what He had done for His people.

I love how the culture of day-to-day Israel was rich in symbolism and meaning that is still relevant today. We have such an expressive and creative God!

You may have already understood some of what was represented in the tabernacle and how it applies to us today. As we study the role of the priesthood, all that this represents should become clearer.

The artist and the priesthood—
our role as priests

When people choose to withdraw far from a fire, the fire continues to give warmth, but they grow cold. When people choose to withdraw far from light, the light continues to be bright in itself but they are in darkness. This is also the case when people withdraw from God.[66] St. Augustine

There were many duties and roles that the priest was required to perform. In the Old Testament, the Levites were a tribe set aside specifically to be priests. For various reasons God's law prevented any other tribe from performing the roles of a priest. They were truly set apart.

The main purpose of the priest in the Tabernacle was to:
- offer sacrifices
- minister to the people
- minister to the Lord
- pray

To sacrifice

We have discussed in brief the brazen altar and how it was used for sacrifice. This typifies the cross. This is where priests would offer animal offerings. During the time of the tabernacle of Moses, this was the only type of sacrifice offered, but David's tabernacle also allowed offerings of praise and worship.

Imagine this picture for a moment: the priests were often covered in blood. It was unattractive. The smell was probably terrible. There was a great deal of mess. There was death every-day for these priests. Blood was on their hands and would have stained their skin and their clothes.

If we truly want to be priests of the King we will need to die. Die to our own dreams for the dream of our King. Die to our own reputation, our own selfish desires. Sometimes it is going to be ugly. It is going to stink. There is going to be a mess.

There will be great sacrifice to follow God and to pursue the calling of God in your life. There will also be great sacrifice to pray. It costs something. It is not going to be easy.

However, just as through the cross Christ rose again in Glory, there is great reward in following the heart of God rather than our own desires. Even though it will come through death, the joy of the cross awaits us!

> John 12:24 *I tell you the truth, unless a kernel of wheat falls to the ground and dies, it remains only a single seed. But if it dies, it produces many seeds.*[67]

Rick Joyner in his book *The surpassing greatness of His power* says: "There is power in sacrifice. The cross was the ultimate sacrifice and it is the ultimate power. The degree to which we will take up the cross daily will be the degree to which we experience the power of God in our daily lives."[68]

To minister to the people

As a priest, or minister of God, your role is to point people to Christ. In the Old Testament, it was only the priests, prophets, kings and elders who were able to mediate between people and God. Christ has now become the mediator for all men, and so our goal should always be to introduce others to Christ. Everything you do should connect people to Jesus. Your songs, your dance, your book, your whole life.

In Exodus 28 we get a glimpse of what it actually means to be a priest and a minister to people. God is instructing the priests on how to dress:

> Ex 28:9 **Next take two onyx stones and engrave the names of the sons of Israel on them in the order of their birth, six names on one stone and the remaining six on the other. Engrave the names of the sons of Israel on the two stones the way a jeweller engraves a seal. Then mount the stone in setting of filigreed gold. Fasten the two stones on the shoulder pieces of the Ephod—they are memorial stones for the Israelites. Aaron will wear these names on his shoulder as a memorial before God . . .**[69]

First, the Lord commands the shoulder pieces to have the names of the 12 tribes of Israel. He then goes on to describe how the breastplates should be made:

> Ex 28:21 **There are to be twelve stones, one for each of the names of the sons of Israel, each engraved like a seal with the name of one of the twelve tribes . . .**[70]

> Ex 28:29 **Whenever Aaron enters the Holy Place, he will bear the names of the sons of Israel over his heart on the breast piece of decision as a continuing memorial before the Lord.**[71]

The priests were required not only to carry the names of the tribes on their shoulders, but their hearts. When you carry people on your shoulders, you are their strength. You are serving them. But when you also carry them on your hearts, you have affection for them, love and care for them. This not only means that you tell people about God, but you also tell God about the people. What a beautiful analogy of the close relationship we can have with our heavenly Father. It also helps us to be aware of our true role as priests—if we are only carrying people on our shoulders or only carrying people in our hearts, we are not fulfilling our role properly.

To minister to the Lord

Another primary role of the priest was to minister to God. In fact, the reality is this is how we grow in knowing God. When we minister to Him, we learn more and more about him because we are spending time with him. The word, minister, in the Miriam Webster Dictionary means to "give aid or service." We serve him with what we have, and with ourselves. This is the most important thing that we can do. Unfortunately, what we often tend to do, especially if we are in some form of Christian ministry, is to become a mediator between God and man.

We can spend most of our time in the outer courts of the tabernacle ministering to the people. There is nothing wrong with loving people and loving what you do, but there is something wrong if that is all we spend our time doing. We can often misunderstand the term "ministry." We can think it means "to serve people," which of course it does encapsulate, but if that is what you are spending most of your time doing, then your life will become out of balance and you will eventually burn out.

Sometimes ministering to people is what we can do when

we are trying to make our ministries known. But there is so much freedom when we walk in our gifts, and let God take us where we need to go. This does not mean that you have no vision for your future, or plan for what is ahead. They are vital signposts for moving forward in your calling. However, they only align with His ways if you are spending time with Him, and talking with Him about where you believe He wants you to go. I am trying to impress upon you the vital need for balance in our lives.

When we place boxes around what we are doing by trying to understand how it all works, we have diminished ourselves and what God can do through us. When we fall into the trap of always serving those around us and never spending time with the Lord, its easy for us just to live out of the gift. Because we are talented and can create, we will still craft beautiful things that will touch people, but there is another sphere for our creativity that can be unknowingly left untouched that is greater than our gift. That is the realm of the anointing. A simple way to explain anointing is to say it is the tangible presence of God on what we do. The only way we can have the anointing grow on our lives is if we are spending private time with God. If all we are doing is serving people with what we have, we can never be "refuelled" by the presence of God.

It is amazing to think that when we spend more time ministering to the Lord, we also have more capacity to minister to others. I find that great surges of creativity and ideas come when I just spend time in His presence.

There were many ways the priests would minister to God. David made sure that there were priests ministering continuously. In the tabernacle of Moses, there were animal sacrifices. In the tabernacle of David, there was also the ministry of the singers and singing (1 Chronicles 15:16–27, 25:1–7), the ministry of the musicians with instruments (1 Chronicles 23:5, 25:1–7), the ministry of the Levites before the Ark (1 Chronicles 16:4,6,37), the ministry of the scribe (1 Chronicles 16:4, 28:12,19), the ministry of clapping of hands (Ps. 47:1, 98:8, Isaiah 55:12), and the ministry of dancing (1 Chronicles 15:29, 2 Sam 6:14, Ps. 149:3, Ps. 150:4), to name a few.

God required the most skilled artisans to work and build the tabernacle. He wanted the best. You only served in the tabernacle if you were at the top of your craft. What a challenging thought for us today when we choose to serve in his Kingdom. Do you give your best to God? Unfortunately there is the misconception by some today, that if you serve in the church as an artist, it's because you can't get a real "gig"! But it certainly was not true in the days of the temple, and it should not be true today. To serve with your gifts within the church should be considered a huge privilege, because God always required the best. We should always keep this in mind when we come to serve. We are not here because we have nothing better to do. We are here because God chooses skilled people to build his temple.

To pray

I believe our primary role as priests is to pray regularly. In Ex 30:7 God gave Aaron instructions when building the altar of incense for the tabernacle of Moses:

> Ex 30:7 *Aaron will burn fragrant incense on it every morning when he polishes the lamps, and again in the evening as he prepares the lamps for lighting, so that there will always be incense burning before God, generation after generation.*[72]

If the altar of incense represents prayer and intercession, then this scripture is signifying that morning and night, Aaron was to pray. Why did He ask this? God is not looking for the five-minute prayer during rush hour. He is looking for communion with us, to share with us in every aspect of our lives. What God is trying to say to us is that if we can start and end our day focusing on Him, we are more likely to spend our whole day abiding in His presence, sharing every aspect of our lives with Him. We have underestimated the role of prayer in our lives. Just as we have assumed priesthood is a role for a select few, we have done the same with prayer.

In Isaiah 56:7 God says His house would be a *house of prayer for all nations.*[73] He did not say it would be a house of worship, or a house of teaching, or a house of healing. Of course, we definitely have all those things and they are wonderful. However, He is expressing that our primary focus should be to pray for others.

As we do this, we also pass on this culture to the generations, so that our children and eventually their children cultivate an atmosphere of prayer and relationship with God.

The Temple of the Holy Spirit

Let us end this chapter with one final tabernacle, the place that God's glory dwells now. When Christ came to this earth the place where God's glory dwelled underwent change. It was no longer in a building. It was Jesus!

> John 1:14 *And the word became flesh and made His dwelling among us . . .*[74]

The Greek word for "dwelt" is "skenoo," which can be translated as "tabernacled." When we accept Him into our hearts,

He dwells inside us. We are in Him, and He is in us. This means that now, in this age, you and I are the temple of God. All the symbolism and richness of the tabernacles of the Old Testament reside on the inside of you!

> 1 Cor 6:19 **Do you not know that your body is a temple of the Holy Spirit, who is in you, whom you have received from God?**[75]

What a huge privilege and an amazing thought. The place where God's glory dwelt was sacred. There was a constant light burning. There was prayer and continuous sacrifice. There were creative ways to express worship to God.

Worship and authority

David was not only a King, he was also a worshipper. He understood that the temple of God needed to be a place of worship. Instruments and choirs grew, and worship became a vital and important part of life. As worship of God was increasing, so was David's authority as King.

Pastor Jack Hayford notes that during the time of the tabernacle of David the boundaries of worship expanded greatly. In his book *Manifest Presence* he states: "As their worship grew, so did their dominion. The same holds true for the church today; it expands in dominion in direct proportion to its worship. Indeed I firmly believe that worship is the key to evangelism."[76]

I believe the Lord wants to restore the church to "Davidic Worship." The heart David had for the tabernacle meant that people could bring a sacrifice made with praise, rather than sacrificing dead animals. It was about sacrificing our hearts! There was a continuous adoration of God. The curtains were gone, there was freedom for all to enter into God's presence—not just the high priest (Hebrews 10:19). The Tabernacle of Moses and the Tabernacle of David were initially in existence at the same time. David allowed the old ways to remain in Moses' tabernacle, and introduced a new way to worship in his tabernacle. What a great representation of the old and new working together. It was not one or the other. It is important that we allow the next generation to bring new ways to old things, yet there is also the freedom for them to work together. We need each other!

You are called to be a King—to have authority, to walk and talk with our Lord as a friend, not just as a servant. You are a bride, not a widow! You are called to have a voice to speak the decrees of God. You are also called to be a priest and bring continuous praise to our wonderful Lord. As a "God artist" let us never take this lightly, because there is great power in it.

The artist, DNA and the power of sound

The power of sound to put an audience in a certain psychological state is vastly undervalued. And the more you know about music and harmony, the more you can do that.[77] Mike Figgis

Understanding how DNA transmits all it knows about cancer, physics, dreaming and love will keep man searching for some time.[78] David R. Brower

*I*n an East African tribe, when a couple wanted to conceive, the woman would go away to be alone until she heard the song of her unborn child. Once she believed she had heard it, she returned to the village and sang it to her partner. When she gave birth, the midwives would sing it during childbirth. At significant events in the child's life, such as puberty and marriage, the song would be sung again. Finally, at the child's funeral, it was heard once more, and it was sung again. It was unique to the child; no one else had this song.[79]

Your unique song

There is a sound, a song that is unique to you. Although this thought could be considered "new age," science is now proving it to be true. You are more than nuclear matter thrown together, made up of blood, bones and cells. There is something heavenly within you that was put there by the Creator Himself.

When you discover the song that is within you, you will gain a greater understanding of the importance of worship, and the importance of sound. Not just in being creative, but in participating in life as a whole. The experience of real worship and honest prayer is effective, fruitful, and brings contentment, peace, greater vision for your life and helps you to draw closer to God.

Sound at the beginning

For us to understand this in detail, I want to share some thoughts on quantum physics, vibration, sound and its connection to worship and the Bible. Do not become too frustrated if it takes a while before you really understand this chapter. It took me a while to understand it too! But I felt it such an important revelation that every God artist should be aware of, and I feel it will help you move forward in creating things that last and have impact.

Let's begin our study in the book of Genesis. Scientist and physicist Dr. Henry Morris, author of *The Genesis Record*[80] gives great insight into how God formed the heavens and the Earth. In Gen 1:1–3 he explains what it actually meant when it said that the Earth was *without form and void* and that God's voice *hovered over the face of the waters*.

The Hebrew word for "hovered" is "rachaph." Translated,

this means "to shake, to move, flutter or vibrate." Physics tells us that there is a vibration at the center of all created matter. This means that all created things—trees, rocks, flowers, and of course humans—have a vibration at their core. If this vibration did not exist, then all the particles that make all things on Earth would just be raw matter. Nothing would have shape or form. Essentially, it would be cosmic chaos. All the elements of creation would be there, yet it would not be formed, because it has no vibration holding it together.

Because all physical matter is represented by a vibration, this also means it is represented by a sound, as all sound has vibration. This means that all created things have their own sound.

In Genesis, when the scripture says that God "hovered," what it is suggesting is that God vibrated over the Earth. If sound is vibration, then this would mean that when He spoke *Let there be light* and His other commands over the Earth, it was His voice that brought order to the formless matter of the Earth. He created the order required to shape it and to bring it into form.

This is very interesting considering that the basis of quantum field theory is that the quantum field (the vibration) is the greater reality than the form it takes on.[81] This means that everything we see is the response to some greater sound.

Hebrews 1:3 . . . *sustaining all things by the power of His word.*[82]

It is His voice that is at the center of all created things. It is His voice that holds everything together and that brings order to us and to the Earth.

Your DNA and its connection to music

Now that we understand that all things are created and brought into order by a greater sound, let us take a look at your DNA.

In 1986, geneticist and biologist Susumu Ohno[83] discovered that he could take DNA sequences in living things and translate them into musical scores. Let me explain this a little further. Strands of DNA each have four nucleotides containing the bases adenine, guanine, cytosine, and thymine. Depending on what the species is, their nucleotides will be arranged in a specific sequence or pattern. Dr. Ohno ascribed a musical note to each of these nucleotides, and because they formed a pattern, much like music forms a pattern or sequence of notes, he discovered that it could easily be translated into a musical piece.

He also discovered that the music became more complex if the organism from which he took DNA was more complex. For example, when he took DNA from a single-cell protozoan, the succession of notes was a simple four-note repetition. However, when he took the DNA of a mouse and translated it into a musical sequence, a section of Chopin's Nocturne Op. 55 No 1 was heard. When he took the cancer cell of a mouse and did the same thing, a section of Chopin's Funeral march was produced. From his many studies, he found that DNA had its own song.[84] Isn't that incredible!

Famous American doctor Larry Dossey, who has also discovered a connection between the spiritual world and the health of the body, said: "The music transcribed from human DNA—for example, the body's receptor site for insulin—is much more complex. Listeners knowledgeable about music have taken these DNA-based compositions for the music of Bach, Brahms, Chopin and other great composers. These melodies are majestic and inspiring. Many persons hearing them for the first time are moved to tears; they cannot believe their bodies, which they believed to be mere collections of chemicals, contain such uplifting, inspiring harmonies—that they are musical . . ."[85]

Each one of us has unique DNA. In the same way that no two sets of fingerprints are alike, no two DNA sequences are alike. Each one of us has our own song and it is different from any one else's. It is yours and no one on this Earth sounds like you. You are more special than you realize!

Your DNA and the breath of God

Let us bring together the idea of creation and vibration, and consider DNA and our song. We will backtrack—God spoke and created order into formless matter. At the center of all living things, there is a vibration. All sound is vibration, which means that at the center of all living things there is a sound.

Now let's talk about singing. When a person uses their voice to produce a note, as their breath passes through the vocal folds they *vibrate* at a certain speed until sound is produced. In Genesis 2:7 it says that God breathed into man, and it was His very breath that brought life to the human body:

> Genesis 2:7 . . . **the Lord God formed the man from the dust of the ground and breathed into his nostrils the breath of life, and the man became a living being.**[86]

It also says that He vibrated over Earth. Breathing, vibration, and sound produce a song. Could it be possible that God *sang* into us and brought us to life? Could it be possible that our DNA is a song because God breathed this song into our bodies, and in a sense imprinted Himself, his uniqueness into each one of us? This idea helps us to see many scriptures in a different light.

> Ps. 40:3 **He put a new song in my mouth, a hymn of praise to our God.**[87]

> Zephaniah 3:17 **He will rejoice over us with singing.**[88]

How incredible to think that the creator of the universe sings over us. That He put a song in our mouth, on the inside of us. Could it be that when we were created, we became a living spirit being when God rejoiced over us with His song? Therefore, could this be why our DNA can so easily be translated into a musical sequence because the core of what makes us who we are was breathed into us by God?

A sad song

As I have considered this idea, it has caused me to wonder about people who suffer from depression, who harbour thoughts of suicide and other turmoil that prevents them from living a fulfilled life. I began to wonder if it is because their "song" is the song of sadness. Were they just created that way?

If you are a person who struggles with life, I have good news for you. If you experience feelings of depression, this is not the song that God wrote for you and placed into you. What life tries to do is to rewrite the song. Situations occur that try to change your original composition. Because the song on the inside of you is a spiritual composition, when life tries to rewrite it, it creates chaos and disharmony. It is then that you will feel ill at ease, unsettled, and emotional turmoil can overtake you. This is not meant to diminish the terrible things that have happened to some people. Life can sometimes be harsh and it can tamper with the sound of who you really are. We can become so used to those struggles that we begin to sing that song. We begin to sound like a funeral liturgy. We have become so used to the new notes and when we live to that tune, we are at disharmony with ourselves. We have dissonance. The chords do not sound right.

What we surround ourselves with: the principle of entrainment

The principle of entrainment is actually what is in force here. At the core of this principle is the universal scientific belief that when two oscillating bodies come close to each other, they will eventually synchronize in harmony with each other.[89] Dutch scientist Christian Huygens founded this discovery in 1656. After inventing the first pendulum clock, he discovered that when he placed two clocks on a wall next to each other, the pendulums would eventually synchronize with each other.[90] What is also behind this theory is that it takes less energy and is much easier for a person or object to align itself with its counterpart than to try to work against it.

The principle of entrainment is found everywhere—in nature, science, biology, psychology, and the arts. For example, a stick floating in a river will follow the current of the stream because it takes less energy than to work against it. Women who live in the same house or work closely together will eventually find their menstrual cycles coincide with each other. Different styles of music have, historically, brought peace and harmony to a troubled soul, or alternatively they have whipped up a crowd into a wild frenzy. This is the principle of entrainment in action. One object eventually aligns itself to the rhythm or vibration of another, because it requires less energy than to work against it.

This is a great analogy for us. The song we sing, regardless of our original theme, will align itself with whatever surrounds us. If you surround yourself with people who are negative, you will be negative. It is easy to find ourselves in this position. Most of the world we live in is full of negative emotions and turmoil. If we are not filling ourselves continuously with the things of God, we will eventually become "in sync" with the world and atmosphere that surrounds us.

What I am trying to convey to you is that at the core of who you are, your DNA, was written and sung with joy. That is why God can rejoice when He sings over us. His song is a song of joy. It is a song of joy because it is filled with purpose and hope for a future life filled with the blessing of God. Do not despair if you find yourself in a difficult situation because hope is written inside of you!

The principle of entrainment also brings home the importance of what type of art we create. We should be aware of the sounds, the words we speak, the dances we create. What effect will it have on people? Can we with a simple work of art, help people to align themselves with God, or dare I suggest, make them turn from Him? We can no longer assume as artists who have a faith in God, that our artistic endeavours are not influential in leading people to the cross, regardless of what type of art we create, and whether or not it is produced in the walls of the church. What you do is not just a "job." First and foremost, we must align ourselves with God, and then aim to produce creativity that helps others come into connection with Him. Again, we find at the core of our creativity we must have a relationship with the great creator.

Finding your song

As you have been reading this chapter, you may be asking yourself, "How do I find out what *my* song is?" This brings us to the reason why we must worship. When we discover the song that is within us, and we begin to sing it rather than someone else's song, there is power in it. We not only connect with who we are, we connect with the person who wrote that song and put it inside us.

Your song is unique. When we sing it in all that we do in our lives, God recognizes it. He recognizes who is singing to Him and His ear turns towards you when you lift up your voice to worship. It is like a beacon to Heaven. God hears your spirit crying out to Him, and He is aware of you because He put that unique song in you. The song turns his attention towards you. When you worship Him, the eyes and ears of God are captured by your adoration of Him. A great lie of the enemy is the thought that God would not hear our deepest prayers or our worship. He does!

It would not surprise me if God has created one perfect symphony by arranging the song that is within each of us to be unique. Imagine if every individual began to live their life according to the song that is in them. It would sound like one great symphony of love to the King. It would be incredible! Maybe each one of our songs makes harmony with every other song. Maybe Africa is the drum section, London is the string section, America is the vocal section, and it all creates one big awesome sound. Alternatively, if you do not sing your song, there is a part in this great symphony that is missing. There is a part to play in God's orchestra, and the gap is obvious when you do not contribute.

Humanism would tell us that for us to be at harmony with ourselves, we should look within ourselves to find that true song. However, it is only when we align ourselves with Heaven, that we will come into alignment with the song's frequency. When we experience God for who He is, we will be influenced by Him; and because He is the creator of that song, we will begin to sing it as it was meant to be. When you worship Him you find out who He really is, which in turn helps you to find out who you really are. If you want to know God more, and if you want to know your song, worship Him!

Corporate worship

Let's explore that thought a little further. If your song is a part of the great symphony that God has orchestrated, what would worship be like in a church setting if we all came with the same intent and with no distraction? What would it be like if we sang about the greatness of God and really focused on the words, instead of going into autopilot when the songs began. A worshipping church is one of the greatest advances against the enemy, yet it is common to switch off because we are so preoccupied with what is going on in our own lives.

Next time you walk into church, try to focus your thoughts immediately on our wonderful God. It is easy for us to walk in with an attitude of, "The worship really does not do it for me," or "I do not really like this music style." We disconnect, thinking we can worship God at another time that is more suited to our style. Without realizing it, this can affect corporate worship. What would happen if every person who was in church was there with the same purpose and same drive to worship?

When the day of Pentecost came in Acts 2:1[91] it says that people came with the same purpose in their hearts. Fire came because of unity and passion to see God move upon them. If we want fire in our services, let's be passionate about seeing Heaven manifest in our midst. It is easy for us not to engage when things are not done our way, or in our style. We need to let go of our agendas and let God's agenda dominate. Sometimes we think too much about how a service is working, and not enough about how we can contribute to seeing the King glorified. I want to let go more and more, even if there is risk involved. I'd rather fail and make a mistake than not try at all and miss God manifesting himself in the way He does in the Bible or in our great revivals. I want Him more than I want what makes me comfortable.

Worship warfare and prayer

When we lift up our hearts to worship God, it is effective on so many levels. We have discussed the power of our song, and the power of our words, yet worship can also be used as an act of warfare and prayer. In fact, worship and prayer go together:

> Rev 5:8 *Now when He had taken the scroll, the four living creatures and the twenty-four elders fell down before the lamb, each having a harp, and golden bowls full of incense, which are the prayers of the saints.*[92]

The harp in this scripture represents worship. The bowl represents intercession. When we worship, the bowl fills. When you worship him, you are interceding and you may not even realize it. Worship and prayer are so connected. I can honestly say that there have been times when worship has saved my life. The best thing we can do for our loved ones and for ourselves in times of trouble is worship because it becomes an act of prayer to our Heavenly Father who loves us and wants to bless us.

The law of lift

The connection between worship and prayer is beautifully explained in Chuck Pierce's book *The Worship Warrior*. In this book, he explains the analogy of a plane and natural laws: "There are two natural laws that oppose each other in the world: the law of gravity and the law of lift. When an aircraft sits stationary, the law of gravity holds it securely to the ground, but as it begins to roll down a runway, the aerodynamics of the wing design causes another natural law to come into play, the law of lift. As the aircraft increases speed on the runway, the two natural laws war until, if the wings are designed right, the law of lift overcomes the law of gravity . . . As the church ascends in worship, the strategies and direction of the Lord in our services are like the law of lift, enabling us to break the hold of gravity on us and open the corridor through the heavenly places."[93]

Therefore, when we worship Him, we begin to rise. As we begin to rise we are confronted with principalities and powers in the air, and we take authority over these things. We clear the way for God's power to flow freely from Heaven onto Earth.

Worship and revelation

The beautiful thing about worship as intercession and warfare is that the very thing we are praying for will become revelation if we persist and do not give up until we receive a breakthrough. It is often when we have broken something in the spirit that we receive revelation for it. For example, we can regularly pray for a situation and not really understand what is happening or what the answer is. However, once we have a breakthrough and an answer to our prayer, we receive a revelation of how to fight in the spiritual realm and win. Once the prayer has been answered, it becomes the springboard for the next time you use warfare in worship. Worship is a training ground for being an insuperable warrior.

When we worship we receive revelation. Worship lifts us up into the presence of God. When we are lifted up into His presence, we will see things from His perspective. When we see things from His perspective, we will pray with His heart in mind. When we pray with His heart, His will is released on the Earth and is manifest in our situation.

There have been times in my life when worship, warfare and prayer did not make sense. You can sometimes feel that you are singing about the goodness of God, His healing power, and power to save when you feel none of these things are happening in your life. Yet there is power in our words and in our praise. It changes the atmosphere, as we have already explained. Regardless of what is going on around us, God's words are truth and He is a mighty and victorious King. Let who He is be made manifest in our praise and to the world around us!

Paul and Silas praised God in a prison cell and it opened the doors and released other prisoners from their chains. Their worship of God caused the jailer to ask *what must I do to be saved?* (Acts 16:25–34).[94] If this is what can happen when we worship God regardless of our circumstances, imagine what it can achieve in us and through us.

Coming to worship our King with our words, as well as our song is *powerful*. Worship changes things, and us. When we sing of the greatness of God, His majesty, and how much we love him, the air is electric with spiritual power to change the world that is around us and to draw us into His spiritual dimension. Imagine this scenario: you connect your song, your DNA, with the power of Heaven's words, and it grabs the attention of God, and changes the atmosphere around you.

Worship and evangelism

I believe that this sound can bring lost souls back to Him too.[95] When we join together and sing, the sound is obvious. It will overtake people by its beauty. If we do not join together and sing it in its completeness, the witness of who Christ is and what He has done for us is diminished. This is why a unified worship team, or a unified church, is one of the most powerful ways we can evangelize our communities:

> Acts 2:1–11 *When the day of Pentecost came, they were all together in one place. Suddenly a sound like the blowing of a violent wind came from Heaven and filled the whole house where they were sitting. They saw what seemed to be tongues of fire that separated and came to rest on each of them. All of them were filled with the Holy Spirit and began to speak in other tongues as the Spirit enabled them. Now there were staying in Jerusalem God-fearing Jews from every nation under Heaven. When they heard this sound, a crowd came together in bewilderment, because each one heard them speaking in his own language. Utterly amazed, they asked: "Are not all these men who are speaking Galileans? Then how is it that each of us hears them in his own native language? Parthians, Medes and Elamites; residents of Mesopotamia, Judea and Cappadocia, Pontus and Asia, Phrygia and Pamphylia, Egypt and the parts of Libya near Cyrene; visitors from Rome (both Jews and converts to Judaism); Cretans and Arabs—we hear them declaring the wonders of God in our own tongues!"* [96]

The first observation from this scripture is that when the disciples were in "one accord" they received the power of God. What is even more enlightening, however, is that it says the crowd came together when they *heard the sound*. The sound is what drew them to what God was doing. Not only that, but regardless of where they had come from *it was a sound they could all understand.*

You know, there are songs we sing in church that people who are not Christians probably won't understand. Yet, if they have the sound of Heaven on them, it will be a sound that goes beyond language and it will reach out to people no matter where they are from. Above everything, I believe all our art should go beyond communication mediums, and our goal should be to find the sound of Heaven that marks everything we do. If we did this, it would not matter what form of expression we used, because if our goal is that the sound of Heaven would permeate it, it will witness of Christ. St. Francis of Assisi said: "Preach Christ, and if you must, use words." The sound is a witness in itself.

If you are not musical

You can worship without being a musician. All you need to do is lift up your heart to him, with intent and purpose. Chuck Pierce makes this great statement: "God is so creative. He presents us with ingenious weapons." To worship him is an ingenious weapon.

Why don't you put this book down right now and begin to worship Him. Thank Him for all He has done. If you need a breakthrough in your life, declare His victory over your situation. Pull out a scripture and begin to speak it, pray it, and prophesy it. Allow the breath of God to flow through you as you sing your unique song to Him. His heart will be drawn to you in a moment, and in an instant, you will find yourself in His presence.

9

The artist and the world

Creative men and women are in the church. Some express their art through music ... but others sit quietly alone, waiting to be affirmed, encouraged, supported. They are waiting for the body of Christ to understand and find room for the novel, the film, the play, the masterpiece ruminating within, that could reach beyond the subculture and challenge the basic assumption of our secular age and point the world to the ultimate truth.[97] David Markee

There are God artists who predominately work outside of the church, and many misunderstandings can make artists keep the church at arm's length. The thought that using your talents within this framework can be second rate—that the church "just does not get it" or that a "real" artist is someone who performs in the secular arena—can easily pass through the mind. As harsh as it may seem, these considerations can often be the truth.

However, if artists continue to remove themselves from the church we will see minimal advances in this area. If we want to see a significant cultural shift, we need to take responsibility to "be the change we want to see." If we keep our distance, feeling frustrated and misunderstood, not only will the church suffer but we will also suffer. I firmly believe we have the power to restore the arts back into it is rightful place—flowing from the house of God.

This will not be easy, as it will require us to be open and accountable to an existing structure that might make us feel uncomfortable. Bringing change to the church will be much harder than working on something on our own. It is not easy to place ourselves in a team situation, where we may not always agree with what is being asked of us. It can be disconcerting if someone comments on our life and makes pointed observations. Often it is easy to feel that we are not being creatively fulfilled, that the focus is to serve a bigger vision, which must accommodate other people. However, if we persist, keep our hearts open and be willing to serve the family of God, I have experienced that we can be rewarded with more creative satisfaction and ideas than we could ever have imagined. At the same time, it is healthy for the artist to help initiate change by being the "fly in the ointment." Sometimes that alone helps bring the reform that is needed for the church to move forward in the arts. Friction can be healthy and fruitful if it is handled correctly and with a heart of love.

God intended for us to use our gifts to serve others and when we do this in greater measure, we will surprisingly feel more fulfilled. It will be a long process and sometimes we may feel that we are walking up hill, yet by investing ourselves into others we find that we are part of something that holds great significance, and influences those who come across our path.

I am not suggesting that all God artists are able to be an

active and regular part of a church's creative arts team. For example, it would not be viable for U2 lead singer Bono to lead worship at his local church every time he was not performing on the road! Every creative person who loves God should be connecting themselves with the body of Christ, investing into it in some way. In return, the church should be loving, coaching, mentoring, and challenging this artist, just as a loving father does with his children. There should be an ongoing two-way relationship, and the artist should always seek out what their contribution could be to this relationship. The God artist is *connected* to God's people.

There are several misconceptions about the God artist who predominately works in the secular arena. This chapter should demystify some concerns. I have also included a section on what the artist can do to integrate themselves into church life, and what the leader of these types of artists can do to love them and help them to grow. I have found that the ideas included in this chapter have worked in my own life, both as an artist and worship pastor.

Ministry vs. entertainment

A common thought that is prevalent amongst Christians is that if art is not directly pointing people to the Gospel then there is no point to it. This is a contentious subject for the artist who is a Christian, yet works outside of the church. If it is just "entertainment" it can make many people feel that what they do is not important or relevant to their faith. This can often lead artistic people away, not from their faith in God, but from being part of a church community, because people see what they do as "entertainment" and consider that it is not relevant within the church context.

When we believe this, we position people into "Christian artist" or "secular artist" categories. Have you noticed that it is not common practice to do both? It is rare to see the rock singer on MTV leading worship at church. However, where it is done, the church thrives. Brooke Fraser, award-winning and best-selling New Zealand artist, is often seen leading worship at Hillsong Church in Sydney. Sun Ho, one of Singapore's biggest pop stars, is also the worship pastor of one of the largest churches in Singapore. The churches in which they are involved are vibrant and there is a sense of great freedom. They are influential, and attract many creative people.

If we create neat little boxes for people to fit into we will always have all our questions answered. Sadly, we won't have a creatively diverse expression of faith, but we will have a safe existence with little controversy. But do we really want to live life like that? It seems to me that Jesus never wanted us to live this way.

It's sad that we often won't embrace the God artist because we have too many questions about why they do what they do. When we do not understand, it is easier to close the door rather than to try to work something out. Therefore, we separate and pigeonhole people because it's easier than using an alternative strategy.

But I believe there is great power in the arts in the church. I also believe there is great power when the God artist brings influence to their industry. When those worlds collide, however, I believe there is even greater power. It is not idealistic to believe that this can happen. Yet, as history has continually shown us, if we embrace this there is going to be a fight. The question here is: are you prepared to fight for it?

An extravagant God

Recently my pastor travelled with American Pastor Bill Johnson to Brazil for a series of meetings. When he came back, he shared with us that in these meetings, diamonds materialized for people who received prayer. One woman wore two silver earrings, and upon receiving prayer, one of those earrings turned to gold. It would be easy to be sceptical about this and my first question to my pastor was: "Why?" Initially, I couldn't see the point of God doing something like this. My pastor responded with a very wise comment. He said to me, "What was the point of Jesus turning water into wine?"

The first miracle recorded in the Bible might appear to be a "useless" miracle because no one was healed or raised from the dead, but it took place so that people could continue to celebrate and to enjoy themselves.

This is a very profound thought: that God would do something because He is extravagant, and because He loves us. In doing so, it may not initially seem that it was pointing people to Heaven, but it does, because it reflects the heart of God.

A similar situation occurs when Jesus says:

Matthew 19:14 **Let the little children come to Me, and do not hinder them, for the Kingdom of Heaven belongs to such as these.**[98]

In this text, Jesus was showing us an example of what it actually means to come into his presence. Children are easygoing. They have no hidden agendas, no world plan, no power struggles. If they want to be somewhere, it is because they *really* want to be there. But the other interesting observation is that children love to play. Why? What is the purpose of playing? What reason is there for them to play? Children play for no other reason than that they enjoy it. It's fun, it's enjoyable, it's what they feel like doing.

When we create art for the sake of creating art, there is nothing wrong with that. It is just like kids playing. It is for enjoyment. It is like Jesus turning water into wine. It is part of the journey, and in its purest sense, when we create like this, with no inhibitions, with no worldview of how we can change things, no evangelism strategy—*we are worshipping*. That is why worship can be one of the most powerful evangelistic tools we can use to encourage people to come to know Christ. We give to God in spirit and in truth, in innocence and playfulness, and in doing so we reveal who God is. What a wonderful way to create, and how freeing to think that we can create beautiful art just because it's part of the journey.

Steve Turner, in his book *Imagine* says: "I do not believe that every artist who is a Christian should produce art that is a paraphrased sermon. A lot of Christian art is for the sake of art. But because art is also a record, it reflects the questions and anxieties of the time, and I would like to see contributions that reflect a Christian understanding of that time."[99]

To be a God artist does not mean that we always produce art that is specifically church-focused, but it never eradicates the responsibility we have to use our gifts with wisdom.

Guidelines for the artist and the leader

The artist

If you are an artist who works predominately outside of the church, there are several things you can do to keep yourself walking the path that God has for you. It will not always be easy, but if your passion remains to serve Him with your life, I want to encourage you to always find the higher road, even when it is the most difficult one.

Conduct yourself with purity

If you are spending a great deal of time around people who do not share similar values, it will be easy to stray away from the truth. The truth can often be more obvious when you are around it all the time, which means it's easy to know right from wrong. It is not always easy to see it when you are not around it. For example, if you are a musician in a band that travels extensively, it could mean you rarely go to church. This could mean the truth is going to be harder to find at times because you are not in an environment where it's being promoted, or where your views are being challenged.

Clearly, it's unacceptable to sleep with multiple partners, take drugs and to do things that are obviously illegal. However, maybe you have noticed that your language is not as pure as it used to be, or, if you are a woman, you find it more comfortable to wear more revealing clothing than you wore in the past.

The entertainment business is different from many other industries. Costumes are important and what you would wear at a show is not what you would wear in church, and that is understandable. A plumber would look out of place wearing his overalls to church as well! If you are in the entertainment business, maybe you are feeling that it is becoming acceptable to be sexually explicit in the way you dress. It's easy to justify to yourself that this is fine because you work in this arena and it is the standard thing to do in the setting. It will feel okay and will feel normal because all around you people act as if it's normal. But it's a fine line between accepting this as the "norm" and working out what is appropriate and pleasing to God, and what is not.

The only way you will be able to conduct yourself with purity is if your relationship with God is not just consistent but thriving. It will not be enough for you to know that you and God are doing "fine." You need to grow, learn, and feel as if you are advancing in your relationship with Him. If this is not happening, then there is every opportunity for sin to seep in through the cracks and into your heart. Sometimes you won't realize it is happening, which is why you always need to be watchful and alert for what the enemy may throw at you. I can remember periods in my life when I thought I was doing well with my relationship with God, but I was not. I was not being challenged in my faith, I was not feeling passionate and experiencing God in a powerful way, yet I was praying and going to church regularly. But true Christian faith needs to be more than that. If we serve a God that turns water into wine, raises people from the dead, can multiply five loaves and two fishes into feeding the five thousand, we should be experiencing God in a powerful way in our day-to-day living. When this happens, it is much easier to live a pure life because our relationship with God is electric and energizes our thinking and our lifestyle. If you are working in the secular arena this approach also allows you to be a witness to those who do not know who He is. It allows you to move in the prophetic and speak directly in situations and people's lives. You will be living an authentic faith, not some cardboard copy cut-out version of the real thing.

Staying accountable

A practical step to keeping your heart pure is to make yourself accountable to people. These people need to be able to speak to you honestly about your life. It is also important that you keep in touch with them regularly. One of the hardest things for creative people who work outside of the church is to stay in touch with a mentor regularly. Catching up a few times a year, or chatting on the phone once a month is not going to be enough to sustain you. What will really help you is if you can make a commitment to chat to someone every week—even if it is just on the phone. I do not feel emails or SMS messages are the most appropriate way to do this because they require no ongoing communication in a conversation style. There really needs to be engaging conversation, where your mentor is asking how you are and you are responding. I tend to feel that emails and SMS messages are easy because they require no immediate response or accountability in the moment.

This type of relationship is not often a friendship. A friend is someone you share life with on the same level. A mentor is someone you look up to, who has attributes to which you aspire, and from whom you feel you can learn. You do not want someone telling you how wonderful you are all the time, even though you should always find an encouraging voice in a mentor. If you can welcome constructive criticism, even when you do not like what you are hearing, you will find yourself growing enormously. Of course, the right person needs to be mentoring you for this type of trust to occur, but you will benefit greatly from this kind of input in your life. Knowing that you have to be accountable to someone will always encourage you to try to live your life with a God focus. Of course, you will also need to have some Godly friends around you who won't be afraid to ask the hard questions. Surrounding yourself with people who share your values, will help you to make the right choices in your life.

> Proverbs 15:22 **Plans fail for lack of counsel, but with many advisors they succeed.**[100]

Quiet time

Another way to keep connected with God's plan is to spend time with him on a regular basis. Finding a regular quiet time can be difficult, but when you have a crazy lifestyle with unusual hours, which is common for the creative person, this is going to be a challenge. You will find if you can keep your quiet time short and that it occurs at the same time every day, there is more chance of it being beneficial. Do not think you can pray for an hour, when you have had trouble most of your life reading scripture for a couple of minutes! Start with ten minutes at a time of day where you know there will be little interruption. Maybe that will be first thing in the morning, or last thing at night. Sit down with your Bible and remember you do not need to read huge passages of scripture for your quiet time to be worthwhile. One or two scriptures on which you spend time meditating will be more beneficial for your spirit than reading two or three chapters. You could start a program where you read a few verses of the Psalms everyday. Try reading different versions of the Bible until you find one that you really enjoy and understand.

I think it is also important to spend time talking with God in an honest way. Share with him how you are feeling, what you are struggling with, and allow yourself to be transparent. Also, allow time where He can speak with you. We do not always have to fill our quiet time with talking and "doing." It should be a time of reflection, where God is allowed the space to speak with you personally.

You may benefit from bringing variety to your quiet times. For example, maybe go for a walk and soak in the surroundings. Talk with God as you walk. Alternatively, find a quiet spot in a park and read your Bible. Some people find a prayer journal or journaling beneficial. I find just turning the TV off and going somewhere in the house where there is minimal sound really centers me. The key here is that you can only give out when you are being filled. You can only live a life of Godly purity if Godly purity is being poured into you. If this is not happening, you will live on your inner resource, but that will eventually run out if you are not consistently being filled by God's presence. Just as you are creative in expressing your gifts, find creative ways to hear from God and spend time with him. You will always lead a pure life when you do this consistently. If you are spending regular time with God, the great artist, you will never be short of creative ideas. You will be tapping straight into the source of creativity in its purest sense.

Understand that it is your responsibility to educate the church

In our own church, we have several professional musicians who graciously invest their time in church events. But it has not always been smooth sailing. There have been misunderstandings and things have not always worked out. Sometimes we as a church have not handled things in the right way, and sometimes the artists' understanding of how things should progress is tainted. There have been opportunities for things to fall apart when this happens. I thank God that we have attracted the kind of people who understand the only way for the arts in the church to thrive is if they persist when there is confusion, and continue to invest into the Kingdom. This means they have to be accountable, that there are times where they will have to learn and submit to the greater vision of the church, even when they may not always agree with it.

It also means the church has had to learn how to work with the artist, to nurture them and to lead them the right way. We might make many mistakes, but we must all come to understand that it is our responsibility to educate the church about the role it has in seeing the arts grow.

Proverbs Pr 14:4 *Where there are no oxen, the manger is empty, but from the strength of an ox comes an abundant harvest.*[101]

I love this scripture because it is saying that by having an ox we have the means to labour the fields. It is referring to productivity. However, with productivity, there is a lot of mess. An ox not only needs a place to sleep, it needs to eat and drink, which means it will produce waste products. Now, who do you think is going to clean up all the mess? Will it be the same person who uses the ox to labour in the fields and produce a desired result? Hint: it will probably be you and me!

So, as we labour the fields and reap the rewards of hard work we must also understand that at times this will create a bit of mess. That mess may become manifest in frustration, or misunderstanding, or offence. Our role is to accept the fruitfulness, yet realize that it falls upon us to clean up any little accidents as well, and not to walk away when the going gets tough.

Do not feel that if you are not around very often that you do not have a part to play in helping the church move into a new level in the arts. If you belong to a church that won't allow you to do this, then maybe that's your "mess" and maybe you are the one who will help turn it around. If you have a heart to serve the local church you will always bless them no matter what. Once you build trust and develop a relationship with the people around you, you will find that they will also be more receptive to your involvement. If you think this sounds like a lot of work—it is! However, the results will be well worth the effort.

Try to be involved in some way in building the church. If your job means that you can't attend regularly, think about what you can do. Focus on feeding the arts in some way. If you can't be on your worship team, for example, learning to develop a relationship with the worship pastor is incredibly important and fruitful. Maybe you could offer to play guitar and lead worship in your home group, or work in the children's church, leading kids in worship. If you come with the attitude of wanting to serve, no matter if it is in a big or small way, you are contributing to church life and that is powerful.

Church view vs. world view

Finally, try to have a well-rounded view of the places where your creative gift can be expressed. History has proven that many times the church has had two separate views of life, and it has ultimately suffered because of it. On one hand, we have the world view which involves scientific advancement, business and money. On the other hand, we have the spiritual and church aspect. History has also shown us that with this dichotomy, the church was not as effective and influential in its community as it could have been. People separated science and religion so much that each view became irrelevant to the other. In today's terms, it could mean that the artist who works in the secular arena feels that they are not "spiritual" enough to minister to people in a church setting. Alternatively, it could mean that a pastor or preacher does not see the "rock star" as someone who could make a significant impact as a minister of the Gospel.

It is easy to de-compartmentalize life into segments like this. If we do this, then we will also think this way about our own church and our gifts. We may think that if we are gifted as an artist who does not produce things within the church context, then we must not be called into the ministry of the church.

It is a challenging ideal to believe that we can be effective artists in several arenas, but it is not impossible. If we can think of what we do as one entity, rather than two separate worlds, we will find it much easier to walk in our calling with freedom.

Some people are strongly and specifically called to the church, and this is effective and what God would require of them. Yet you will find that those people who have great influence in the church have also had influence in the world and the attention of the media. The point to make here is: be confident that God has called you to something, then walk boldly into it keeping your heart focused on what God would want from you.

You may have noticed in this book that I have tried not to use the term "Christian artist." Instead, I have coined the phrase "God artist." This is because I see an artist who loves God as someone who is able to influence whatever medium they choose to walk in, whether that be in the Christian world or not. As God artists, we need to understand that we are able to work in many different scenarios. Instead of thinking that we are only accepted or effective outside of the church, we must also understand our gifts can fit within the church context. It is never one or the other, it is both.

When we begin to think like this, so many more opportunities for God to move through us will open up. We will also experience great freedom and release in the arts as we open ourselves up to it's possibilities.

The pastor/leader

If you are a pastor or leader of artists who work outside of the church the next few thoughts may help you. From my experience as an artist, and also as a leader in the church, I can say with confidence that your guidance and pastoral care can leave lasting change, and have great impact, in the lives of those you lead.

Relationship

Firstly, develop a relationship with those you lead. If the only time you meet is when you need to reprimand them or to use them for a special service or event, they will not feel that you are caring for them. This may result in them not allowing you to speak into their lives. This kind of relationship may be difficult because it requires you to be a challenging voice in their lives, without being condescending or judgmental. I heard someone say, that "rules without relationship leads to rebellion," and it's a completely true statement. If the only time we are talking to people is when we need something, or need to bring discipline, we are not going to help them grow into what God wants them to be.

These kinds of relationships can be difficult to cultivate, especially because most pastors and leaders are extremely busy and have many people to care for. Couple that with the artist who travels a great deal, and communication between them can often be sparse. What I do in our church is to try to make sure that if I can't spend time with them then one of our key leaders will. It also helps if more than one person from your team is keeping in touch and developing a friendship with them. They are more likely to stay connected if they sense they are being genuinely cared for, and loved and accepted by the church.

Once you have established a good relationship, you will find it will be much easier to mentor people. We must always do this with a loving heart that does not come from a place of judgement. This may be difficult, especially if you notice things in people's lives that you know are hindering their progress in some way. However, we do not need to rush in terms of their growth. I find that if I am unsure of how to handle a situation in someone's life, if I am patient, quite often, just loving them helps them to see the changes they need to make. We should trust God a little more! We do not need to come up with all the answers, we need to love and guide as best we can and God will do the rest.

Their involvement in church

If you have creative people in your church who are quite successful and are working hard, be careful that you do not overuse them. It is easy to make use of these people, because due to their efforts our events reach a high standard. From the church's perspective, this is wonderful because it means we can serve our community with excellence, but we should be aware of the potential for burnout. Some of the questions I often ask myself are: "What event can I have them participate in that will have the most impact on the community?", "How can they be involved at a significant level, yet in a way that will not overwork them?", and "What is the best use of their time?".

For example, you may find having them involved in a Christmas service to be more fruitful than in a mothers' group morning tea. Both events are important, but a Christmas service will be a larger service that attracts more of the community. For the organizer, both events require a great deal of work, but for the same amount of effort the Christmas service may be able to reach more people because of the excellence an artist can bring.

Here is another example. Let's say you have a full-time photographer (we'll call him Matthew) in your church who has won many awards and has held several exhibitions. For a while, you have wanted the media arts department in your church to grow. One way you could do this would be to hold an exhibition of photographs during a conference, or over the Christmas period, or at the end of Sunday services. If Matthew is involved, you know the level of excellence will be of a high standard.

So, you ask Matthew if he is interested in becoming involved and he readily agrees; he has always wanted to contribute to church life and in this way he feels he can contribute.

You ask him to run the whole event and to have most of his photos on show. It is likely to be a very successful event and everyone in the church is delighted that Matthew is involved. However, this event requires a tremendous amount of work for Matthew. Because the church has never undertaken anything like this before, Matthew does everything himself, from advertising, to hanging up the pictures. He is happy to do this because he wants to help the church. Yet as he prepares for the exhibition, he finds he is also very busy with his own work. He completes the church job well, but at the end, he is very tired, and wonders if he should commit to something like that again. He has worked on things that are not his passion, such as advertising and hanging up pictures. Because the church is new to something like this, he discovered that in order to make the exhibition a success, he had to do many things himself.

Now, let's change the scenario a bit. Instead of asking Matthew to run the whole event, you invite him to a meeting where you share your ideas for a media arts exhibition. He has some amazing suggestions that you write down and know you can implement quite easily. Then you assemble a team that can carry out all the preparation. Someone who is gifted with administration is happy to look after correspondence with other artists in the church. They send emails and ask people to present their photos to Matthew for submission in the exhibition.

Someone assists Matthew with the hanging of the photos in the foyer. Another person organizes the advertising for the event. Finally, you ask Matthew if he would be interested in being the patron for the day, with one or two of his photos being featured in the exhibition. The event is a big success.

The difference with the second example compared with the first is that Matthew enjoys the latter experience and would be happy to help out again. Other people who are gifted in different areas are brought in to play a part; other artists are given an opportunity to show their art and to grow by having the experience of working with someone as experienced as Matthew. He feels he has contributed to the life of the church and looks forward to the next time he can become involved. He finally feels he has found a place within the context of church life, and he has made some friends and developed some key relationships. It was not easy, and it was still a lot of work, but Matthew was working in His gift, and the church was growing its arts team at the same time.

This all looks so simple on paper, but of course, what happens is that when we lose the *reason* for what we do, we face the danger of not using people wisely. When we stay focused on the cause, we will help people. In this instance, we want to see Matthew integrated into church life, yet we also want to grow the media team. We also want to see a church have an impact within its community. If we lose sight of the cause, we see Matthew as a way to raise the profile of the church. The community is certainly impacted, but there is so much more we can achieve when we stay grounded in loving and helping people when we create programs and ideas.

Honesty

When we do not understand the life of the artist in the world, it is okay to be honest with them about it. I am convinced that people do not expect the church to have all the answers, yet that's what we try to do. Being honest is important in developing a relationship, especially when it is done out of a heart of love. There have been times when I have not understood some choices my peers have made. It would be easy for me to judge them based on my own experience, and I certainly have at times. I hope that as I grow into my role as a leader, I am accepting of whom they are right now, yet also wise enough to base my beliefs on what the Bible really says, not what I think it says. This may at times take a great deal of prayer and many "bumps in the road" as you work together to understand each other.

I will never forget when I joined the staff at my church. I was (and still am) a touring artist. I asked my pastors if they wanted me to stop touring so that I could focus on my role more specifically. They saw that I was really energized when I travelled and ministered in other churches. The most precious thing for me is that although I thought they would expect me to limit my touring, instead they encouraged me to continue doing it. My senior pastor said to me, "We are all new at this. I don't know how we are going to make this work, but let's go on the journey together and learn together." To be honest, I was quite surprised that a senior minister of a large church would admit that he did not know how we would make it work. He was honest enough to share his feelings, and this has empowered me to be all I am called to be.

On the journey so far, I have discovered several things. One is that I can do a lot more than I thought was possible. I have also discovered what works and what does not work. We have had moments where we have all agreed some things are not working, but it is such a blessing to me that he allowed me the freedom to try things out. Because of his honesty, I felt free to be myself.

Now that I am no longer worship pastor, I am still very much a part of the worship team. Because of honesty, we have been able to continue a healthy relationship where we journey through life's changes together.

If life was black and white it would be easy to know what was right and wrong. But there are just some things we will not be able to discern immediately. It is only when we pray and go on the journey together that we sometimes find the truth in a situation. When the focus is on relationship and loving people, not on what is right and wrong, we come to better conclusions about how to handle the grey areas.

However, there are some things that are not acceptable. Someone who poses nude in magazines is probably not a good choice for leading worship at church! Yet even then, you can love them, befriend them and guide them on the journey. It really is true that *love never fails* (1 Cor 13:8).[102] I am a firm believer that people change significantly when they are loved, far more than when they are judged.

Connection

Your role as a leader is to make sure people are well connected in the family of God. This is important, because it will be difficult for them to do this if they are frequently absent. Often in church life, things become incredibly busy and the friends we make are only those people we see all the time. Out of sight can mean out of mind and this means that relationships can dwindle. This makes it much easier for the artist to be disconnected when they are at home. Again, we see that relationships are the foundation for helping the artist thrive. Finding ways that they can become involved is one way you can help them stay connected. For example, maybe there is a home group with which you feel they would connect, or you could let them know when special services take place that they would enjoy.

Recently I sent an email to a friend who is in the USA and often travels as a musician. When he is around, he will play keyboards at church although it is difficult for him to be involved on a regular basis. I chose to retain him on the roster because I wanted him to feel connected and he has a great heart for the church. Because he was away, I sent an email letting him know what we did at rehearsal so he felt like he did not miss out. Given that his life is so busy, it would be easy for me to think that he would not be interested in what we are doing in Australia. However, within minutes I received an email back saying he appreciated the fact that I let him know what was happening. He even asked how he could be involved when he came back! Keeping people connected will really help them stay plugged into the local church, where God brings so much satisfaction to their life.

How they are involved?

It's important for the church to use the artist in the right context. For example, I have a good friend who is a well-known theatre star. One of the things she does not feel comfortable doing regularly is leading worship. If I am going to ask her to be involved I would not ask her to lead worship for a special event, but I would ask her to perform a song, or contribute in a way that makes the best use of her gifts. I believe when people do what they love doing, they are the best ministers they can possibly be. If I tried to make her fit a mold that better suits my agenda, I do both of us an injustice.

You may find that some artists are interested in trying something new. If you are confident that they can do this well, then this is wonderful. Good communication is important in finding out what works best for you, the artist and your church.

A final word for the leader

It may appear from the above discussion that what you are doing is trying to accommodate artistic people. I understand that at times it can seem that all you are doing is trying to make people happy. This is not what I am suggesting. What I am trying to point out in this chapter is that there have been misunderstandings that have caused us to develop mechanisms that help us to "hold our ground." To protect what you have can seem genuine, but I do not believe it's the most productive way to work together. Artistic people certainly are different. They are more sensitive than most and often have their identity wrapped in their ego. I know because I have been like this and I'm sure you have too! My encouragement to you is always to look for new and inventive ways to embrace the artist. Your church and you personally will grow because of it.

A final word for the artist

You are valuable. What you do is worth something within church walls. If you have felt hurt by the church, I want to ask you to do something that will be difficult. Let it go and try again. Do not give up. *God wants you in the church.* He wants you to feel a part of a vibrant community of believers who are using their gifts to make a difference. I know you already make an impact, and there is great fulfilment in investing your time into the body of Christ. For some of you, this is going to be heartbreaking. A number of old hurts and many frustrations may resurface, but I guarantee that it will be worth it.

I also want to challenge you to try some new things within church life. For example, maybe you have always wanted to be a worship leader but felt your skills were stronger in performance or acting. Do not let your lack of confidence or experiences regulate your choices. Be open to God, you will know deep down in your heart what He is really calling you to do. Relax and just do it! You may make mistakes but at least you gave it a go. You may even surprise yourself.

PART
TWO

The artist and history

10

Introduction

*We are made wise not by the recollection of our past,
but by the responsibility for our future.*[103]
Bernard Shaw

As God artists we often know little about those artists who have gone before us and what influence they have left behind. In our passion to see God glorified through our gifts we have unknowingly failed to look back into our past. Everything is about moving forward, making a mark, leaving a legacy. To look back could be considered foolish, pointless and unproductive. There has often been the unconscious thought that anything that does not have its place within the context of the Bible is secular and thus should be avoided.

Yet there is so much to learn from our past. When we scour the history books, we find out where we have come from, why we do things the way we do, and discover hope and wisdom to make an impact on the future.

When was the first creative act birthed? What has shaped the arts since the beginning of time? Why do we think the way we do? Where does music come from? What has remained in our culture that we have brought down from the centuries, and more important, why? Are there common struggles throughout history that the artist has had to face, and still has to face? Where is God in all of this? What is my responsibility as an artist today in light of this? Can I learn from the successes and mistakes of others and become a better artist? These are some of the questions that prompted me to write these next few chapters.

I am not an historian, and one section of a book could never encompass the complete history of world art. However, I have endeavoured to pinpoint historical facts that are relevant for the purposes of this study. There was so much I could have written, but it would have required writing another book, one much better left to the experts of art history! The knowledge I impart to you here is solely for you to gain insight into our past and discover where we have come from. In doing this, you will learn to understand where we stand today, and what you can do to leave a mark for the future. I pray you will see the greatness in the lives of people mentioned here and also their humanity. I pray that it will give you courage to rise up and be more than you thought you could be.

For the purpose of this study, I have mainly focused on European history. This is because many of our philosophical and artistic endeavours have been influenced enormously by European culture. Asia, Africa and the Arabian empire have had their own unique and beautiful culture in philosophy and art but I have primarily focused on the "common thread" that links each of the centuries into one another. This is not to say that these cultures have not contributed to who we are today (because they have), but rather that western society is mainly based on European thinking and culture.

I mainly discuss music, art and literary achievements because historically these mediums have been quite influential in our society. I have not looked at all forms of artistic expression—such as dance and opera—because the field is so diverse and I could not possibly cover all facets of the arts in this book. However, if they are of particular interest to you let me encourage you to make further studies in these areas. Also, I have provided a brief outline of some of the most interesting people who have shaped our history.

After you have read these chapters on history, I will discuss some key points about what we can learn from the past. I hope that as you read, your mind will be enlightened through learning and that some of your questions will be answered.

11

In the beginning

There is geometry in the humming of the strings, there is music in the spacing of the spheres.[104] Pythagoras

Employ your time in improving yourself by other men's writings, so that you shall gain easily what others have laboured hard for.[105] Socrates

In Heaven before the world began

*I*n timeless space, before the universe was created, God existed. In our world bound by time frames, it is hard to comprehend that God is and always will be eternal. Even though we may never fully grasp this truth this side of Heaven, there is comfort in knowing that all that we see has been created by a matchless God who is not restrained by the limitations of timelines. We cannot put a history marker at His beginning, because God was here before the beginning. However, from what we know from the scriptures, we can get a fair idea of how His artistic nature has influenced and shaped our world. To do this, we need to look back to the time before our world was created.

In the beginning, before our world was birthed, there was music in Heaven. There are many opinions about the following scriptures, and I would like to share my thoughts in the following paragraphs. In Ezekiel 28 we catch a glimpse of Satan's role in Heaven as the chief worshipper:

Ez 28:13b–14b . . . *The workmanship of your timbrels and pipes was prepared for you on the day you were created. You were the anointed cherub who covers* . . .[106]

Lucifer is another name for Satan. The name is derived from variations of the Hebrew word "helel" that means "light bearing one." This scripture intimates that he was not only musical, but that he has music in him. He had timbrels and pipes built into him. He was also "the anointed cherub who covers." He covered the throne of God with worship. His role was to bring the praises of God around the throne of God.

In Is 14:12–15, before the creation of our world, we learn that he fell because he became proud. He said to himself:

Is 14:12–15 *I will raise my throne above the stars of God.*[107]

It says in the scriptures that he was cast out of Heaven by God, and a third of the angels also rebelled with him.

Now, let me pose a question to you. If Lucifer was the angel who covered the throne of God with praises and he is no longer there, who fulfils this role? Who covers the throne of God with praises? Apart from the other angels that are still in Heaven—it is us! When we worship God with our prayers, life and music, we cover the throne of God with praises.

In light of this, it is easy to understand why there is a great battle, as old as the ages, for the arts, and in particular music.

Lucifer was a skilled artisan, a skilled musician who has fought to be king over the arts in our world. We are his greatest threat, because we fulfil a role that he once fulfilled—to cover the throne of God with worship.

Today when you watch music clips and listen to music that is dark or explicitly violent or sexual, you can see how Satan has tried to twist and deform something that should have been used for the praise of God. Music was intended to worship Him, and Satan has done all he can to try and remove music from worship since he fell from Heaven. When we worship God in spirit and in truth through our creative gifts, we restore the arts into its rightful place.

Throughout the centuries, as we study the lives of many who have left their mark, you will begin to see the struggle man has had in carrying this huge responsibility, often fighting with the very thing that was Satan's downfall—pride.

In the beginning—the creation of the worlds

> Gen 1:1 *In the beginning God created the Heavens and the Earth.*[108]

Job says that there was music at the dawn of creation:

> Job 38:4 *Where were you when I created the Earth? Tell me, since you know so much! Who decided on its size? Certainly you'll know that! Who came up with the blueprints and measurements? How was its foundations poured, and who set the cornerstone, while the morning stars sang in chorus and all the angels shouted praise?*[109]

Our world began with the arts. I find it incredible that singing and shouting surrounded the creation of the world. We serve a very creative God!

600–500 BC Early philosophy

Pythagoras (circa 580 BC–500 BC) was one of the first known philosophers. He was considered a great mathematician and scientist, and was one of the first to think that the Earth was round, that every planet had an axis and that all planets travelled around one central point.[110] These were quite significant discoveries considering that there was no technology that could yet prove this to be true.

Of Greek descent, he recognized the connection between numbers and music. This idea was widely accepted by all men, including those who believed in the one true God. Through the study of astronomy and biblical references to Heaven, Pythagoras, and eventually Plato, believed that the planets through harmonious movement created music in the cosmos. It was widely accepted in this era that astronomy and music were linked together. This concept was called "the music or the harmony of the spheres."

The Roman philosopher Boethius wrote in the 6th century: "There are three types of music. The first type is the music of the universe, the second, that of the human being, and the third type is that which is created by certain instruments . . . Now the first type, that is the music of the universe, is best observed in those things which one perceives in Heaven itself, or in the structure of the elements, or in the diversity of the seasons. How could it possibly be that such a swift heavenly machine should move silently in its course? . . . It is impossible that such a fast motion should produce absolutely no sound, especially since the orbits of the stars are joined by such a harmony that nothing so perfectly structured can be imagined . . . Thus there must be some fixed order of musical modulation in this celestial motion."[111]

Pythagoras believed that all types of music—the music of the universe, the music of the human being, and the music of instruments—were linked and part of a system that was ultimately sustained by God. Therefore the thought was that everyone should be striving to create music that was harmonious with the universe. In the words of Andrew Wilson-Dickson, author of *The History of Christian Music*, to do this "would thereby form a part of God's great symphony of proportions."[112] This great discovery, became somewhat lost as evidence and faith in science replaced mystical thought. However, advances in technology have expanded the study of the universe, which has revealed that harmony and music does exist within the planets and throughout the known universe, probably more so than our early philosophers and free thinkers could have ever imagined.

Socrates and Plato

Socrates (circa 470–399 BC) is our most well-known philosopher.[113] Born in Athens, Greece, he had many students, his most notable being Plato (circa 428 BC–348 BC). Socrates' philosophy had a great influence on his society. He encouraged the youth of his day to think for themselves, to question what they were taught and to make their own decisions. Ultimately, this led him to his death as it was thought that he was corrupting the minds of the youth.

Although we have none of Socrates' writings, the words of his student Plato were recorded. Not only was Plato a writer,[114] he was also a thinker, great mathematician and philosopher. He founded the Academy in Athens, and the Institution for Higher Learning, which was the first of its kind in the western world. He kept records of Socrates' teachings that are still valued today.

12

Bible times

History, despite its wrenching pain, cannot be unlived, but if faced with courage, need not be lived again.[115]
Maya Angelou

4000 BC–200 BC Old Testament

Throughout the Old Testament, creative arts plays an important role. However, because its history spans more than 4000 years, it is difficult to capture all the cultural shifts in art mediums. Because of the large time span, the changes were wide and varied. We do know that lyres, harps, and tambourines and timbrels were used, as well as trumpets and many other instruments. It has been suggested by many Bible historians that King David invented thousands of instruments.

Singing features many times in scripture. Dance and percussion were also common. It seems from what we know in scripture that the music of the common people was spontaneous, joyful and emotion filled.

Music in the temple, however, was performed by the most skilful musicians.[116] It was not as free form as the music of the common people because there were rituals to be followed. The Talmud and the book of Ecclesiasticus from the Apocrypha describes the worship for the day of atonement, which included 12 male singers, supplemented with young boys to add a sweet sound.[117] There were also cymbals and trumpets. Other instruments included 9 or more lyres, harps, and between 2 and 12 cane pipes and cymbals. There is evidence that some of these instruments were, at times, played very loudly. There are sources in the Talmud that say that from the temple they could be heard all the way to Jericho.

The Bible also talks about a song being evident at the foundation of the temple (Ezra 3: 10–11).[118] The Lord commanded the barren woman to sing (Is 54:1–5).[119] When Jehoshaphat led his army into battle, it was the musicians who went out first (2 Chronicles 20:21).[120] We also know that Saul asked David to play for him to bring him peace from tormented spirits (1 Samuel 16:14–17). Clearly music was an important part of life in early biblical times.

New Testament

As most of the early Christians were originally Jewish, we find that many cultural similarities remained in Christian worship and the arts.[121] Initially, Christianity did not take on a completely new culture, but rather adapted Jewish tradition into its new beliefs. This could be why there are not many documented records of the arts during this time as most of it was a long-standing tradition taken from a life that most reformed Jews already knew. Therefore it did not need to be recorded, as it was part of common life. Musical notation was not invented until around the 10th century, so there was no way of recording music except by passing it down through the generations and by singing it.

1st century

Most theologians agree that the birth of Christ was between 4–6 BC.[122]

During the reign of Nero AD 54–68[123] Christians were punished by gruesome deaths (mostly as spectator sport), although they were peaceful pacifists. Christians and their faith were a threat to the status quo; they were thought to be conspiratorial. Although its followers were persecuted, the Christian faith spread rapidly from outside Palestine to Greece, Gaul, Egypt, Syria and Rome.

This is where the first versions of what we call Christian art was birthed. Early Christians took pagan symbols and gave them Christian meanings. As they were meeting secretly after the resurrection of Jesus, this was a way they could alert fellow Christians in a relatively safe manner.

The symbol of the fish is an example of this, and was used to alert other Christians that they also followed the fisher of men.[124] The fish, which represented Jesus, also represented the last supper, and baptism by water. The word for fish in Greek, also provides the initials of the title Jesus Christ, Son of God.

Other symbols included the cross, the good shepherd, the dove, the lamb, and the four evangelists, representing Matthew (as a man), Mark (a lion), Luke (an ox) and John (an eagle). All these symbols had deep meanings and were often only understood by Christians, and used as a means to alert other believers of their faith without rousing the attention of the authorities.

13

The early church

The bee is more honoured than the other animals; not because she labours, but because she labours for others.[125]
Saint John Chrysostom
Faith is to believe what you do not see; the reward of this faith is to see what you believe.[126] Saint Augustine

2nd century

The 2nd century was both an exciting and troubling time for Christianity. The many different factions of the church and the vast growth of Christianity meant there was diversity in what was considered to be Christianity. The traditions and culture of each nation also influenced what people believed.

During this era, we find the influences of many people whose thoughts, philosophies and actions changed the world. Cai Lun (circa AD 50–121) from China, invented paper. The great thinker Ptolemy (circa AD 90–circa AD 168), a mathematician, geographer, astronomer, astrologer and philosopher, lived in Egypt and was of Greek ancestry. Among his many scientific pursuits, he also wrote a music theory work, *Harmonics*, which explained the theory and mathematics of music. He based musical notes on mathematical equations. Another term for this is "Pythagorean tuning" as it was first discovered by Pythagoras and later changed and expanded by Ptolemy. The era also produced Juvenal the Roman poet, who has inspired many authors with his writings in *The Satire*, which criticized Roman life in a comical yet critical way. People were beginning to be influenced by these philosophical thinkers and cultural change was beginning to take place.

3rd century

Rome was the center of the civilized world, and was marked with prosperity and affluence. The 3rd century was a time where this power was challenged and many wars were fought by a seemingly all-powerful Rome. The arts flourished, and Roman power was unrivalled. In AD 264, the introduction of gladiatorial combat in Rome was where many Christians met with their death after being fed to lions in front of a bloodthirsty audience.

4th century

Edict of Milan

The Emperor Constantine of Rome (AD 280–337) converted to Christianity, which ended the persecution of Christians. Worship leader and singer/songwriter Ray Hughes notes an interesting point on the power of worship in contributing to the demise of the gladiatorial combat: "Christians were frequently thrown to the lions as a source of Roman entertainment. The Christians believed deeply in their hearts in worshipping God with song. As the lions rushed into the arena to devour them, they would stand boldly and lift their voices and sing praises to their God.

These songs were so powerful and anointed, the violent roar from the crowd turned into a hush so the lyrics could be heard. Time after time, as these Christians would be thrown to the lions only to release a song before their death, it became such a moving and awesome scene that it simply lost the sense of victory and sport for the barbaric audience."[127]

In AD 313, the Edict of Milan was signed which changed the face of Christianity in the world. This edict declared that all religions would be tolerated throughout the Roman Empire. Some historians have called this era "The peace of the church." Christianity was no longer illegal and no longer needed to be hidden. Christians were free to worship openly, many took positions of authority in the community, and churches were even allowed to own their own property.

Yet apathy was still prevalent in Roman life. Even though Christianity became a legal religion, most people lived the way they had lived before. According to Christian theologian Frances Schaeffer, this apathy also permeated the art of this era: "Officially sponsored art was decadent, and music was increasingly bombastic. Even the portraits on the coins became of poor quality. All of life was marked by the predominant apathy."[128]

The first Christian Bibles were written. The Greek Bible manuscripts *Codex Sinaiticus* and the *Codex Vaticanus* were produced. It is said that Emperor Constantine commissioned the writing of these Bibles.

Constantinople

In AD 328, Emperor Constantine built a new city in the east— Constantinople. This city became a beacon for learning and Christian culture. Beautiful buildings held grand ceremonies with rich worship. Many visitors travelled far to visit the "Hagia Sofia" or "Divine Wisdom," considered one of the most breathtaking buildings in the world. The city eventually held more the

500,000 people, surpassing the population of Rome, which had dwindled down to a mere one-tenth of this figure.

Christians in many different countries began to worship in languages other than Greek. In places such as Spain, the Celtic countries and Gaul, Latin was spoken for worship. Eastern countries such as Syria used Arabic, Byzantia, Greek, Egyptic and Coptic. Today, influences from these languages are evident in our own worship culture. Passed down from Rome, Latin remained the most common language of prayer and became Europe's most commonly shared language for almost 2000 years.

Theodosius I, the Roman Emperor from AD 379–395 made Christianity the official state religion of the Roman Empire and banned pagan worship.

Christians began building more handsome and larger places for worship, as they no longer needed to be hidden. Among the basilicas built during this time are Old St. Peters in Rome, Church of the Holy Sepulchre in Jerusalem and Church of the Nativity in Bethlehem.

St. Augustine

St. Augustine (AD 354–430) of Hippo is considered one of the leading theological fathers of the reformation of salvation and grace.[129] *The Confessions of St. Augustine* is thought to be the first autobiographical work of western civilization, and became a model for other Christian writers over the next 1000 years. He also wrote *City of God*. He was a great theologian and thinker, and well respected by Christians and non-Christians alike. His views on time (that God exists in the "eternal present") and the human ability of memory were influential in western thought. Many famous sayings have come from St. Augustine's writings, including "Love the sinner and hate the sin," "Heart speaks to heart" and "To sing once is to pray twice."

Another of St. Augustine's interesting views was that the

Bible should not be taken literally if it contradicts God-given reason and science. Wisely however, he told people that knowledge of scriptures, in particular the creation story and redemption, were certainly difficult to understand and that they should be prepared to change their views and opinions as new information was brought to light. He was considered a humble man, willing to learn and reshape his own ideas as he learned, and a man honest about his failings, having struggled with lust throughout his whole life. This was a topic he wrote about and he hated himself for this side of his character.

St. Augustine's definition of what classified a hymn was accepted by many into the 5th century. However, it was Bishop Ambrose of Milan who encouraged change. From biblical times into the 5th century, hymns consisted of scripture. However, Ambrose led the way in writing hymns made up of words and lyrics that were freely composed.

Luther and Calvin would rely heavily on his teachings, and St. Augustine is considered the forerunner to the Reformation.

The fall of the Roman Empire

There is much debate as to the true reason behind the fall of Rome. Some suggest it was due to lead poisoning in the water supply, while others declare that soil exhaustion and erosion depopulated the Roman countryside. Some historians point to the rise of Christianity, and even to the ill-fated invasion of the Huns and other raiders as reasons for the decline. However, it is quite evident that there was political and governmental unrest within Rome, and this is widely considered the true reason behind its demise.

As the Roman Empire grew, it gradually became more difficult to abide by the laws of one ruler, and power struggles against Roman generals caused weakness within the government's rule. The Western and Eastern empires split in two in the late AD 300s. The last ruler of Rome was Romulus Augustulus, who stepped down. The West Roman Empire was divided up and the East Roman Empire became the Byzantine Empire. The influences of the Byzantine Empire on art, language, architecture and law still exist today.

The breakdown of the Roman Empire created civil unrest, wars, and many rulers came and went. Financial breakdown occurred as merchants no longer felt safe to travel to Rome for trade. Thus, the change from the ancient world into the medieval world began.

5th century

As the Empire began to crumble, it was inevitable that the fall of Rome would occur, and this took place in the year AD 476.

Illuminated manuscripts

The first illuminated manuscripts were discovered during the 5th century. They are manuscripts in which the text includes decorated initials, borders and miniature illustrations. The earliest surviving illuminated manuscripts are from the period AD 400 to 600. They mainly originated from Ireland, Italy and other parts of Europe. From these manuscripts, we have a keepsake of the culture and heritage of places such as Greece and Rome.

Old manuscripts, including the Bible, were copied and recopied in the monasteries. This allowed much of the knowledge of European culture to be preserved.

Mosaics

In the 5th century, mosaics adorned buildings in great measure. Byzantine art was a term used to reflect the art of the middle ages (which began from the 5th century). During this time, mosaic art became characterized by structure, symbols and icons. Realism was replaced with people's own ideas and concepts of spirituality. This was good in one sense as it showed that they were looking for greater spirituality and meaning, but with its increase came the demise of the portrayal of nature and humanity. This was such a contrast to the art found in early Christian catacombs, for example, which depicted in simple form, real people and real life.[130]

The Byzantine Church in the eastern portion of the Roman Empire (and eventually the west) was characterized by light and color. An example is Hagia Sophia in Constantinople, which was consecrated in AD 537.

Pope Leo the Great

As Rome's power started to flounder, we see the church beginning to be involved in the politics of the city, and great leaders emerged. Pope Leo the Great (AD 440–61) successfully negotiated Atilla the Hun's retreat across Europe. He was a very wise diplomat and because of Popes such as Leo, the church began to increase in power.

6th century

Gregory the Great (540–604)

Building on the strength of the church in terms of political power was Gregory the Great. A great leader, he did much to build Rome to be greater than its former glory. Not only was he a committed Christian, but he rebuilt the aqueducts of the city, developed a welfare system for charities and hospitals and revised the tax system. Much of this was put in place by the clergy. He also wrote and preached on faith and Christian matters. He had an understanding that there needed to be clear patterns to follow in terms of the belief system of the church for worldwide unity.

Part of his desire to see the whole church unified crossed over to his views on worship. He tried to encourage conformity on this matter in all countries. Different Latin liturgies, such as Celtic, Ambrosian, Gallican and Mozarbic, started to find their way into Rome. Today, we can still hear the Mozarbic liturgy in the Spanish cathedral of Toledo, and in the northern Italian cathedral of Milan the Ambrosian Liturgy can still be heard.

It was not until the 10th century that music was notated, so we have no record of many of these changes. However, thanks to medieval scholars inventing apocryphal musical deeds we have some basic records of some of these liturgies. The term "Gregorian chants" is the name given to a collection of liturgical chants that accompanied the celebration of Mass and other ritual services.

Other significant artistic endeavours took place during this century. The oldest (and still surviving) illustrated biblical codex was written. This is called the *Vienna Genesis* and is an illuminated manuscript.

Taliesin (circa 534–circa 599)

The only known poet from this era is of Welsh origin—Taliesin. Legend tells us that he was the Chief Bard of Britain. At 13 years of age, it is said that he prophesied in exact detail how and when King Maelgwn would die. His works explored religious, mythological and shamanistic themes, the last named featuring control over spirits, weather and illness, as well as astral projection. A book of poems, *The Book of Taliesin*, was written in the Middle Ages, about 1275.

7th century

Even though the Eastern Roman Empire continued to experience decline, Constantinople still grew to be the largest and wealthiest city in the known world. The Islamic religion started in Arabia and by the end of the 7th century the Koran was collated by followers of the prophet Mohammed.

It is also believed that the first book of English poetry was written in the 7th century, by Caedmon (658–680). Appropriately, this poem was a hymn on the Creation.

14

Arts around the world and the Dark Ages

Man thinks, God directs.[131]
Flaccus Albinus Alcuinus (circa 735–804)

8th century

We have mainly focused our study on art in Rome, as this city was considered the center for learning and creativity. However, over the centuries we begin to see the huge influence on the arts from Asia, England, and of course, other parts of the world.

Asia

In Asia, Du Fu (712–770) from the Tang Dynasty was thought to be the greatest of all of the Chinese poets. Considered a "poet historian" by Chinese critics, his works were initially little known, but eventually became influential. Military tactics along with the rise and fall of governments were expressed through what are now considered historical poems.

Another well-known poet from the Tang Dynasty was Li Bai, also known as Li Po (701–762). More than 1100 of his poems remain today. Heralded as "The Poet Immortal," western culture discovered his works through translations of versions of his poems by American poet Ezra Pound.

England

In England, Flaccus Albinus Alcuinus (circa 735–804) a scholar, ecclesiastic, poet and teacher, had a great love for poetry, even though he was troubled by the idea that some of the greatest poetry was written by non-Christians.

He studied at the York School, a place that considered arts, literature and science to be as important as religious studies. Today we have several of his manuals and educational works and several theological and commentary biblical works. He also wrote many poems, including one that included the history of the church in York.

When Alcuinus was 50 years old, he travelled from New York to Europe to become Charlemagne, King of Franks (742–814), advisor and head of the palace school at Aachen. Charlemagne invited singers from Rome to his court and created a school of song. It is because of Charlemagne's encouragement of scholars and the arts that artistic expression flourished once again. Interestingly, all of his scholars were clergy.[132]

9th century

The next few centuries were known as "the Dark Ages." During this time there was little creative endeavour and a loss of classical art forms. Political unrest, and many economic problems, meant there was little room for creative focus. The Roman Catholic

Papacy was one of the few organizations that had international power, but it was limited due to poor communication between European regions. History was preserved thanks to the Catholic monks who tirelessly kept records of the past. However, because only a small percentage of the population could read and write, it was difficult to share the knowledge.

During this era, art was predominantly created because the Catholic Church needed it for their church functions. For example, cups, vessels, crucifixes, rosaries and statues were required to adorn mass services and buildings.

10th century

The 10th century is part of what we now call "the Dark Ages." However, although this period of artistic decline may have been true for Europe and China (where there was growing political change), places such as Islamdom and Spain were growing in culture and were in their prime. The Byzantine Empire was also flourishing.

The invention of musical notation

One of the most significant achievements of the 10th century was the invention of musical notation. Guido of Arezzo—an Italian Monk (circa 991–1050) was regarded as its inventor. He also invented the "solfeggio"—the Do-Re-Mi scale. Up until this time, music and words were sung from memory, which meant that legacies of the past were passed down from person to person. Initially this was acceptable, but as the artistic world grew and more music was written, it was difficult for people to remember such vast amounts of music. There were other methods of remembering music before notation was invented by D'Arezzo, but these were mainly in the form of signs placed above words that served as a reminder for the singer. There was no instruction regarding how long to sing notes, for example.

Not only did this development allow music to be passed down from generation to generation, but more could be written now that it was not necessary to commit songs to memory. We also see the birth of more complicated and diverse songs written by many more composers. What a loss we would have today if notation had not been invented and we had no record of some of the incredible hymns we can still sing hundreds of years after they were written.

15

The rise of the arts once again

Seek not to understand that you may believe, but believe so that you may understand.[133] St. Augustine

11th century

The Great Schism of 1054 split the church into two schools of philosophical, religious and liturgical understanding. However, despite this split the 11th century it still considered the turning point out of the Dark Ages and into a century of great change for Europe. There were Gregorian Reforms, which dealt with the independence and moral integrity of the clergy. The first crusade occurred in 1095, its main aim being for the church to reclaim the Holy Land. Between the 11th century and the 13th century there were nine major crusades and much bloodshed. Yet during such upheaval and change, the church seemed to revive, and the arts once again began to flourish.

In other parts of the world, important literary achievements were achieved. In Japanese literature, *The Tale of Genji* is not only considered a classic work, but is possibly the first novel ever written. The oldest major work that we know of from French literature is *The Song of Roland*. Written in the literary form that was popular in the 11th and 15th centuries, it was a style of poetry that expounded and celebrated the great deeds of a hero.

Saint Anselm (1033–1109), The Archbishop of Canterbury from 1093 to 1109, was an Italian philosopher and theologian. He is called the founder of scholasticism, which was a method of learning that combined classic ancient philosophy with medieval Christian theology.

12th century

The 12th century bought the emergence of "mystery plays." Performed by both amateurs and professionals, these plays were developed to represent stories from the Bible. Although their origin is not completely known, they became very popular during this era. By the end of the 15th century, these plays were sometimes performed on highly decorated carts that travelled around cities. Performances would often go on for several days. Special effects sometimes accompanied liturgical text as the people re-enacted major events in the church calendar, such as the death and resurrection of Christ, but on other occasions the events were performed with completely plain and stark backgrounds. The variety of poetic and theatrical styles within a "mystery play" could be quite spectacular.

Architecture also began to flourish during the 11th and 12th centuries. Buildings often associated with Romanesque and Gothic architecture are church buildings and cathedrals. Gothic architecture in particular was birthed in France with the building of the Saint-Denis Abbey in 1140. This style is represented by large high windows, which supplied streaming light from on high, and pointed arches.

The years between 1100 and 1300 saw the emergence of the troubadour (which means inventor or finder). Troubadours hailed from southern France and were often aristocratic musical poets who paved the way for secular music.

13th century

In the 13th century, we see the "motet" emerging through music culture. Motet is a term used to refer to varied choral and musical compositions. The best way to describe a motet is as a piece of music in several parts that includes words. The Medieval Latin word for motet is "motectum," which means "different voices moving against each other."

The earliest forms of motets were discovered during the 13th century, but its flavour was captured beyond the Medieval period to Renaissance and Baroque music. During the Baroque era, Bach wrote six motets as far as we know. Antonio Vivaldi is another composer who wrote in motet form. Later in the 18th century, Mozart wrote the well-known *Ave Verum Corpus* in motet form, although fewer artists were writing in this genre by this era. By the 19th century, German artist Johannes Brahms composed in motet form. Many of these compositions were performed acapella-style, or with the organ. English versions of the motet are sometimes called anthems.

Manuscripts

In the 13th century, manuscript culture began to develop, and the writing of manuscripts spread to the cities. Before this time, monks in monasteries were the main people who wrote manuscripts of religious text as a means of storing information. As we see the move to the cities, an increase in jobs for making, copying and trading of manuscripts began, as well as a rise in universities regulating them.

Before printers were able to mass-produce books for a large audience, scribes wrote manuscripts that were commissioned by wealthy people. During the 13th century, enough rich people could afford to have specific manuscripts printed. It became a huge trade and kept scribes in business. Paris was one of the first cities to have a successful trade in the production and sale of manuscripts for the rich people who wanted them. It is hard to imagine today how precious the printed word must have been in the 13th century. How much we take for granted!

By the middle of the century, the Pecia system of copying books developed in Italian university towns and was eventually taken up at the University of Paris. The Pecia system allowed the copying of manuscripts to take place much faster, by breaking up books into several sections that could be rented out by individuals for copying. For example, if there were 30 or 40 Peciae, it meant that 30 or 40 students could be copying excerpts all at one time, rather than one student trying to copy a whole book.

By the end of the 13th century, wooden movable type was created and printing as we know it today began to take form. In 1298, Chinese governmental minister Wang Zhen invented a moveable type system using metal type letters to print. However, it was not until 1470 that the move away from hand printed books began. Paper began to be preferred to parchment and the printing industry began to embark on a radical change. Manuscripts were still written and illuminated into the 16th century, but they were mainly for royalty and for use on special occasions.

Universities throughout Paris, Orleans, Montpelier, Cambridge, Oxford, Naples, Padua, Salerno, Salamanca, Toulouse, Coimbra and Lisbon also began to emerge and provide education.

Thomas Aquinas

As we study the Renaissance in the next chapter, it is important to point out the influence of Thomas Aquinas leading up to the 14th to 16th centuries. Aquinas (1225–1274), a Dominican, studied in the universities of Naples and Paris and was the great theologian of his day. His thoughts on humankind had great impact on the Roman Catholic Church and even today he is considered by many Catholics to be the church's greatest theologian and philosopher, while his influence on western thought in general is considerable.

His belief was that at the fall of man, the will is corrupted, but not the intellect; therefore, human wisdom could be relied upon in much greater measure. This allowed people to mix their opinions and ideals with the thoughts of philosophers, in conjunction with the teachings of the Bible. Naturally this resulted in a convoluted view of the true message of the Gospel.[134] It also meant that the church had more authority than the scriptures.

The benefit of Aquinas' teaching, however, was that more importance was placed on man's place in this world, and his purpose. This also began to show in the art of this era. For example, some Gothic sculptors began to carve figures in a more natural state.

16

The Renaissance

Every block of stone has a statue inside it and it is the task of the sculptor to discover it.[135] Michelangelo

I saw the angel in the marble and carved until I set him free.[136] Michelangelo

It had long since come to my attention that people of accomplishment rarely sat back and let things happen to them. They went out and happened to things.[137]
Leonardo da Vinci

14th century

The Renaissance

It is no accident that the period between the 1300s to the 1600s was called the Renaissance period, which literally means "rebirth." Rich patrons began to commission artists to complete paintings and sculptures for their homes. The Roman Catholic Church was a huge benefactor for commissioning artistic endeavours. Artists were becoming more financially viable, setting up studios and hiring assistants and apprentices. The emphasis was on artistic endeavours and learning. Interest in anatomy and the human form—the body, mind and soul—became the focus of the artist in sculpture, painting, music, architecture and art. There was an understanding that the greatest creation was humankind, and all artistic pursuit was aimed at studying it in every aspect.

It is also no surprise that during the Renaissance period—this "rebirth" of culture and study—we not only saw growth in culture, but in the reformation of the church. By the 16th century music in particular was about to embark on an incredible transformation that influenced the whole of Europe. Scholars such as Wycliffe (1320–1384), the first person to translate the Bible into English, allowed the scriptures to be read by the common people. Famous reformist Martin Luther challenged the Catholic Church, and the Reformation Movement began.

Although this was a time where the arts flourished, with the Renaissance also came a strong humanistic element. The church began to move away from the simple doctrines of the early church and became distorted. This eventually divided European thought between the humanistic elements of the Renaissance and the Bible-based teaching of the Reformation.[138]

This was also the century that saw the birth of the great poet and writer Dante Alighieri. Born in Florence in Italy, W.B. Yeats called him "the chief imagination of Christendom."[139] T.S. Eliot said: "Dante and Shakespeare divide the modern world between them.[140] There is no third." Dante was famous for his work *The Divine Comedy*, which although a poem, was written in similar vein to C.S. Lewis' *The Great Divorce* and John Bunyan's *The Pilgrim's Progress*. Unfortunately, Dante followed the same train of thought as Thomas Aquinas; that is, he often mixed humanist views and philosophy with Bible-based teachings, which meant his expression was a mixture of all three.

Other great writers of this era included Italian scholar and poet Petrarch, sometimes called the "Father of Humanism," and Boccaccio, Italian author of the *Decameron*, whose translation of "Homer" from its original Greek became one of the keystones of the Renaissance, bringing Greek literature to life after a seven hundred year hiatus.[141]

Music was also incredibly important in the Renaissance, and huge advancements were made not only artistically, but also technically. In 1501 Ottaviano Petrucci in Venice printed music sheets with the use of moveable type, while orchestration became more detailed with the creation of the homogeneous sound of the Renaissance. This eventually led to the emergence of opera in Florence.

15th century

Michelangelo (1475–1564), the famous Italian Renaissance painter, sculptor, architect, poet and engineer, was considered arrogant, a perfectionist, and was rarely completely happy with his works. As with many artists of his day, he became an artist against his father's wishes.[142] His two most respected sculptures, the *Pieta* and *David*, were created before he was aged 30. He believed that in every block of stone was a statue and that his role was to discover that statue.

He was often commissioned by the Roman Catholic Church to provide sculptures and paintings for their churches, tombs and shrines. His paintings included the famous *Creation of Adam*, which along with many other images was painted on the wall of the Sistine Chapel in Rome. His painting of the ceiling of the Sistine Chapel took four years to complete. Another of these works is the tomb of Pope Julius II (which took 40 years to complete due to constant interruptions and features Michelangelo's statue of Moses). The tomb is located in the Church of St. Pietro in Vincoli in Rome.

Some of his paintings and sculptures were considered

sacrilegious and obscene because they depicted nakedness. Even after his death his work remained controversial, in particular his painting *The Last Judgment* on the wall behind the altar of the Sistine Chapel. Eventually, his apprentice was appointed to paint over the genitals of naked people in the painting.

In 1546, Michelangelo was appointed architect of St. Peter's Basilica in the Vatican, and designed its dome.

Humanistic ideals often permeated Michelangelo's art. For example, it could be assumed his sculpture of David was of King David from the scriptures, except that the sculpture is of an uncircumcised man. It is thought that this sculpture represents the idea that man is a God—perfect, strong, in control and in waiting for his destiny.

As he grew older Michelangelo softened his views and this was reflected in his artwork. This was probably because of the influence of Italian noblewoman and poet Vittoria Colonna, who embraced the ideals of the Reformation.[143]

Leonardo da Vinci (1425–1519)

Leonardo di ser Piero da Vinci[144] (1452–1519) was an Italian polymath: scientist, mathematician, engineer, inventor, anatomist, painter, sculptor, architect, musician, and writer. (I wonder what he did with his spare time!) He is probably considered the greatest inventor who ever lived. Some of his most famous paintings are the *Mona Lisa* and the *Last Supper*. He also drew *The Vitruvian Man*—a renowned picture of a naked man with his arms and legs outstretched and standing inside a circle and a square.

As an engineer, da Vinci conceived ideas that were vastly ahead of their time. Conceptually, he invented a helicopter, a tank, the use of concentrated solar power, a calculator, a rudimentary theory of plate tectonics, the double hull ship design, and many others. Few of his designs were constructed (or were feasible to construct) during his lifetime. Some of his smaller inventions, such as an automated bobbin winder and a machine for testing the tensile strength of wire, entered the world of manufacturing unheralded.

He greatly advanced the state of knowledge in the fields of anatomy, astronomy, civil engineering, optics, and the study of water (hydrodynamics). Of his works, only a few paintings survive, together with his notebooks, which contain drawings, scientific diagrams and notes.

Francis A. Schaeffer, in his book *How should we then live?*, points out that the Renaissance eventually lived up to it is name. Although the church embraced humanistic thought, the benefit of the Renaissance—apart from its art forms—was that there was a change of thinking about humankind. Man began to look at himself in a different way, and of course, this was expressed in the arts.[145]

Some people believed humanistic thought to be the final word on the state of humankind, but there were many who held the scriptures as the final and absolute word. John Wycliffe (circa 1320–1384), who produced the English translation of the Bible, was one such man.

To this day, we can see both patterns of thinking—the humanistic values of the Renaissance, and the scriptural truths of the Reformation—influencing the whole world.

17
The Reformation

I am not of the opinion that all arts are to be cast down and destroyed on account of the Gospel, as some fanatics protest. On the other hand, I would gladly see all arts, especially music, in the service of Him who has given and created them.
Why should the devil have all the good music? [146]
Martin Luther

The first thing I ask is that people should not make use of my name, and should not call themselves Lutherans but Christians. What is Luther? The teaching is not mine. Nor was I crucified for anyone ... How did I, poor stinking bag of maggots that I am, come to the point where people call the children of Christ by my evil name? [147] Martin Luther

As the Renaissance Movement promulgated thoughts of humanism, at the same time a movement with opposite views began to emerge in northern Europe. The Reformation was born thanks to people such as Bible translator John Wycliffe, who believed the Bible was absolute, and others like John Huss of Bohemia, who believed that the scriptures were the final authority and that Christ was the only way to find salvation. But as the era of the Renaissance was coming to a close, it was Martin Luther who was considered to be the leader of the Reformation.

The Renaissance Movement thought that everything started with man. That is, all the answers we needed were inside of ourselves, that the mind was not fallen, only the will. This way of thinking about humankind was based on a mixture of the scriptures, the works of the philosophers, and human thought. Nevertheless, the Reformation had a healthier view of the fall of man—that we could not start with ourselves and that human thinking alone was not reliable. Only through what Christ did on the cross could we be saved, and the scriptures were the final authority—not the church.[148]

16th century

Martin Luther (1483–1546)

In the 16th century, the Reformation led by Martin Luther, monk, theologian, priest and professor, transformed the church and changed western civilization for ever.[149] Luther was adamant and passionate in his views, questioning many beliefs of the Catholic Church, such as the teaching and sale of indulgence, devotion to Mary and Purgatory, and the ultimate authority of the Pope. The life of Luther is truly one of a man who shook the whole world.

Luther translated the Bible into German, and wrote many works that were popular in his day. His best-known work, *The 95 Theses*, was nailed to the door of the Castle Church in Wittenberg. This writing, which questioned many of the beliefs of the Catholic Church, spread throughout Europe within a two-month period, thanks to the invention of printing, which

Luther saw as God's gift to help him spread the true message of the Gospel.

He doggedly questioned the man-made traditions of the Catholic Church, understanding that no one could earn the righteousness of God, and that to repent in faith was the only way to receive the favour of God. As the Catholic Church was pardoning sins for a fee, both to those living and dead (rich relatives hoped they could help their unbelieving or sinful relations by paying large sums to the church), Martin Luther's claims advocated freedom to the poor who could not afford these indulgences, and this caused uproar within the church. As Luther spread the message far and wide, many towns throughout Europe had a huge spiritual awakening, finally feeling as if God was on their side and true freedom from condemnation and sin could be experienced.

As a monk, Luther was accustomed to prayer, and had a love for music. He was trained as a singer and lutenist. He wrote several hymns, the most famous being "A Mighty Fortress is our God," and was a catalyst for congregational singing within the Christian Movement. His desire to see the common people worship God meant that he used simple melodies—children's songs, folk songs and carols and changed their words so that ordinary people could more easily worship. He understood the power of music to touch the deepest part of the human soul and desired that all experienced it: "Next to the word of God, music deserves the highest praise. . . . Whether you wish to comfort the sad, subdue frivolity, to encourage the despairing, to humble the proud, to calm the passionate, or to appease those full of hate, . . . what more effective means than music can you find?"[150]

Today, almost seventy million Christians worldwide belong to Lutheran churches, and four hundred million Protestant Christians can trace their roots back to Martin Luther. His German translation of the scriptures allowed the common people, not just clergy, to read the Bible for themselves. It is this translation that later became the foundation for the King James Bible.

Luther's life was also mired in controversy, with what some consider his anti-Semitic writings about Jews, something the Nazis widely promoted in Germany from 1933 to 1945. Again, we see throughout history that passionate endeavours by great men are no easy task, and that no one is perfect or without contradiction. Many mistakes were made, but a return to the scriptures and examples set by the early church did emerge and opposed the views that Renaissance humanism had created.

The Counter-Reformation

Unfortunately, even though change and freedom was coming to the church, the great leaders of this new era could not agree on the simplest theological matters. Thus, the Counter-Reformation took place in the mid 1500–1600s, in opposition to the Reformation began by Martin Luther and with resistance from the Catholic Church. This caused what was known as the Thirty Years' War, which at various points involved most countries in Europe.

Great men such as Luther, and other reformers such as John Calvin (born Jean Cauvin)[151] and Huldrych Zwingli, were all passionate about their beliefs when it came to the Eucharist and other doctrinal matters. These differences crossed over to art and art forms. Calvinistic churches held their strong belief in pre-destination, and did not allow any decoration in their churches as they felt that decoration could distract people from true worship. The folk songs of Martin Luther were unacceptable, and John Calvin believed that only music that had the New Testament and Psalms as their foundation could be played. Singing in harmony was not widely accepted and the use of choirs was replaced with the singing of the whole congregation that was unaccompanied by instruments. The Lutheran Church, on the other hand, continued in the richness of German musical tradition. In fact, classical composer George Frideric Handel was the grandson of a Lutheran clergyman and Johann Sebastian Bach wrote almost all of his compositions while working as a Lutheran organist, cantor and director of church music.

Yet, even though Calvinistic teachings seemed to be austere, a great movement of worship occurred. The professional musician Louis Bourgeois[152] was commissioned to set the Psalms to music. Because of the immense restrictions put upon him by the Calvinist Church, a rich and simple work was created—the famous *Genevan Psalter* (1562). The music was memorable and well written, because it had to be. The impact this work had on the Christian world was huge, and it was translated from its original French into several different languages. Its characteristics have inspired and influenced many hymn books worldwide. Again we see imperfect men, and imperfect ideas, still being used by God.

It would be an understandable assumption to think that the Reformation was *against* art. Many sculptures and artworks were destroyed because religious symbols were idolized during this era. In fact, it has been documented that donors of these cult images were often the very people who destroyed them because they represented unbiblical worship. Many people of the day had a change of heart as they returned to their first love—a relationship with Christ.

In fact, the Reformation did much to encourage art. We have already mentioned the beauty of the *Geneva Psalter*. Luther himself was a great songwriter, musician and singer. And we must not forget that the music of Bach (whom we will discuss in the next chapter), was brought about by the effects of the Reformation. As Schaeffer so aptly put it: "There would have been no Bach had there been no Luther."[153]

18

The Baroque era

The aim and final end of all music should be none other than the glory of God and the refreshment of the soul.[154]
Johann Sebastian Bach

17th century

The 17th century is commonly known as the Baroque era. Baroque is a term that comes from the Portuguese word "barocco," which means "wild" or "untamed." In music, this is a term used to identify music that is mood driven. In jewelry, it was used to refer to an uncut stone. It certainly identifies the arts of this period.

There was vast diversity in Europe in terms of architecture, music and art. This was measured by grandness and drama. Rembrandt (1606–1669) was one such grand artist and painted hundreds of works of art. All his pieces reflected drama, high emotion and mood. He often painted religious scenes, including *Christ Preaching*, *The Three Crosses* and *The Jewish Bride*. Although he had many flaws (as we all do), it was obvious through his paintings that he believed in the truths of the Gospel and had a relationship with Christ. This is evident in his painting the *Raising of the Cross* (1633), where we see a man in a blue beret helping raise Christ up on the cross. This man is Rembrandt himself—aware that it was his own sins (as much as yours and mine) that placed Christ there.

Even though Greek and Roman texts were considered the basics in education, the Reformation increased the desire for classical learning. In the period 1500–1600, there was great advancement in astronomy, medicine, physics, and the arts. Poet Jean de La Fontaine, as well as producing great poems, wrote his famous "fables."

The debate began to roar, with people arguing that writers of that time were far superior to those of the past. As the hunger for learning grew, science also began to advance. Up until this point science was generally a mixture of what the philosophers of early centuries, in particular Aristotle, taught by "observation" rather than "experimentation." People rarely questioned their beliefs and the church ingrained the thoughts of the philosophers into their culture.

With the invention of the telescope in 1609, Galileo was able to document his findings through experimentation, not just observation, and suggested that some of Aristotle's thoughts about the universe were not correct (much to the horror of the church who asked him to recant his findings during the Roman Inquisition in 1632).

What is interesting here is that most scientists of the day had a Christian worldview as their foundation for scientific study. Even though not all these scientists were Christians, for many, the basis of study was that a rational God created a rational universe, so it made sense that through observation and experimentation, rational conclusions about the universe and ourselves could be found. For example, Sir Isaac Newton (1642–1727) became known for his groundbreaking theories on gravity and sound and produced some of the most influential writings of the age. Centuries later, both Alfred North Whitehead (1861–1947) a mathematician and philosopher, and J. Robert Oppenheimer (1904–1967), suggested that modern science was birthed from a Christian worldview. Francis Schaeffer puts it beautifully: "We must never think that the Christian base hindered science. Rather, the Christian base made modern science possible."[155]

It also seems that the separation between philosophy, science, art and religion was not as wide as it is today. In fact, Francis Bacon wrote in 1620: "Man by the fall fell at the same time from his state of innocence and from his dominion over creation. Both of these losses however, can even in this life be in some parts repaired; the former by religion and faith, the latter by the arts and sciences."[156]

This was an era where most Christian musicians worked for local churches, rather than performing for secular audiences. Great artists such as Antonio Vivaldi (1678–1741), Johann Sebastian Bach (1685–1750), hymn writer Isaac Watts (1674–1748) and Rembrandt led the way. Composers Bach and Handel are great examples of God artists who were passionate about using their gifts to glorify God. In doing so, their art witnessed of their faith and continues to do so today. Let's take a look into their lives to gain a picture of what a God artist looked like in the 17th century.

Johann Sebastian Bach (1685–1750)

It seems from what we know of Bach[157] that he was driven to write music that strived for excellence in the church and in glorifying God. He sought to have skilful musicians and singers glorifying God inside church walls. This often brought him great frustration, because he often felt that what the church stood for and what he was writing were two different things.

Like many composers of his day, he strongly believed that

music had the power to move people, not just for joy, but to express sadness, pain, or anger. The trend of composers of this era was to express different emotions by different musical ideas. These emotions were called "Affekten"—affects or moods. Bach seemed to reflect this style within his music more than his contemporaries. Unfortunately, the church did not agree with his idea of presenting music, or the fact that he did not often write music that had biblical text at its root. His unique style can be heard in his highly emotive cantatas, which combined his own poetic language rather than those of the scriptures. He often wrote songs that were his interpretation of sermons. Although this was unique in his day, it was very powerful and personal, reflecting his love and the revelation of his experience of God. The fact that his music and his name are still well known is evidence of this, and more than 200 cantatas remain today. Bach was often at odds with the church, but it is clear that he was passionate about God and his desire to move people through his music.

George Frideric Handel (1685–1759)

Born in Germany, Handel was already showing talent at eight years of age, when he played an organ postlude after a church service and his father encouraged him to take piano lessons.[158] By the age of twelve Handel had written his first composition and was proficient on the organ. He could also play the oboe, violin and clavichord.

However, after his father died, he entered law school because that is what his father requested. Even though his passion was music, he tried his best to please his father, who would not have approved of him becoming a composer. Eventually he abandoned his studies to give himself completely to music. After travelling to Italy and working for several years in Germany and Italy, he then moved to England where he spent the rest of his life.

He had many setbacks over the course of his life and went

bankrupt several times. He was liked by some monarchs and disliked by others, depending on their personal musical tastes. He constantly competed with English composers and was faced with audiences that were hard to please (if they even bothered to turn up to his performances, that is). He spent most of his life trying to rebound from financial difficulties, which eventually led to him becoming ill, and he determined to give up music altogether. He was attacked by his local church for writing religious works that were to be performed in secular places for secular audiences (*Esther and Israel in Egypt*, for example).

He was an eccentric yet humble man. He often wore a white wig with curls hanging around his shoulders, and could swear in several languages. Handel was always able to keep his sense of humour even during difficult times.

In April 1741, he gave what was to be his final concert. The financial pressures had left him in so much debt that he could no longer continue. At the age of 56, he became so discouraged that he could see no other option but to retire. Then a good friend and benefactor, Charles Jennings, gave Handel a libretto based on the life of Christ and taken completely from the Bible. He was commissioned by a Dublin charity to write and perform a work for a performance benefit. Four months after what was to be his final performance, he set to work on a piece that would leave an indelible mark on musical history.

From all historical accounts, it appears that he barely left his house for almost three weeks. He became so engrossed and inspired that he worked relentlessly and tirelessly, rarely stopping to eat. One day a friend came to visit Handel and found him sobbing because of the emotion he was feeling for the work. It is recorded that Handel quoted St. Paul during this time saying, "Whether I was in the body or out of my body when I wrote it I know not." In just 24 days, he completed more than 260 pages of orchestrated manuscript. This work is, of course, the famous *Messiah*.

Messiah was performed first in April 1742 at a charitable benefit, a year after what was meant to be his final performance. This performance alone raised enough money to release 142 men from a debtors' prison.

Still surrounded by speculation and controversy, Handel began performing *Messiah*. Amazingly, his financial situation began to improve. Even during his lifetime, the work became standard repertoire for other composers who were influenced by Handel's incredible talents. Handel personally conducted more than 30 performances of *Messiah*, raising a great deal of money for charity at benefit concerts.

One biographer noted: "*Messiah* has fed the hungry, clothed the naked, fostered the orphan." Another writer said: "*Messiah* has probably done more to convince thousands of mankind that there is a God about us than all the theological works ever written."

However, Handel's words are probably the most poignant. After the first performance of *Messiah* Lord Kinnoul congratulated Handel on providing the audience with excellent "entertainment." Handel replied: "My Lord, I should be sorry if I only entertain them, I wish to make them better." [159]

A man who loved God, he was often seen in church on his knees in devoted prayer.

He gave to charities even during times of financial hardship and was an optimist who trusted that God would make all things work together for good.

He was attacked by the church, yet he remained faithful to his art. Even after *Messiah* became a well-known and accepted piece, some church figures spoke against his work. In fact, John Newton, composer of the traditional hymn *Amazing Grace*, preached every Sunday for a year against secular performances of *Messiah*. Handel never spoke against his attackers, and although discouraged at times, always continued doing what he believed he was born to do.

19

Romanticism and science

Catch on fire with enthusiasm and people will come for miles to watch you burn.[160] John Wesley

I was cut off from the world. There was no one to confuse or torment me, and I was forced to become original.[161] Joseph Haydn

Neither a lofty degree of intelligence nor imagination nor both together go to the making of genius. Love, love, love, that is the soul of genius.[162] Wolfgang Amadeus Mozart

18th century

Romanticism was a movement prevalent in the late 1700s to the mid-1800s. Beginning in Germany and England, it moved the arts away from classicism, focusing on self-expression and experimentation. There was a focus on the individual and the appreciation of nature.

The Augustan Age was a term given to the early 1700s in England, where satire was a common writing form. Jonathan

Swift wrote *Gulliver's Travels* and Alexander Pope was famous for his poems such as *An Essay on Man* and *The Dunciad.*

The era was also called the Age of Enlightenment, or the Age of Reason. The focus was on science and rational thought. Many of the thoughts birthed in this period were the foundation for the leaders of the American and French revolutions.

It was a time of great change in the world. The Industrial Revolution began in Britain and spread through Europe and North America, and as machines and factories were manufactured at a much faster pace, capitalists, business leaders, bankers and investors thrived, while lower class workers became poorer. Many people migrated to cities to find work, which resulted in overcrowding and poor living conditions. Today we can see the benefits of the Industrial Revolution, but also its disadvantages, with an increase in pollution on land, and in water and the air.

In the previous century, the music of Bach and Handel was complex and represented Baroque and Rococo styles. With their death and the emergence of new musical artists, we see simplicity, restraint, and balance. Composers Mozart, Haydn and Beethoven reflected this style, with the use of the melody line being the emphasis, with supporting harmony lines and a greater scope for dynamics. The piano was introduced, the modern symphony orchestra was prevalent and the standardized sonata form was popular.

Ludwig van Beethoven (circa 1770–1827)

One of the greatest composers of this era was Beethoven. Born to an alcoholic father and a sickly mother, Beethoven's early life was one of adversity.[163] He was naturally gifted at a young age, but because of his circumstances was never encouraged to learn or grow in his musical gifts. He was born and baptized as a Roman Catholic. As a young man he moved to Vienna where, despite an inclination to be crude, he was widely accepted by the aristocratic world for his piano performances. He was not as refined as his audience. He was considered clumsy and ill-mannered, and he had no interest in changing to try to impress them.

Beethoven had a foul temper and had frequent outbursts of anger. He was a misunderstood and lonely man. He never married, although it was not by choice. He was drawn into deep depression as he grew older, mainly due to his deafness. He tried to hide it from the world as much as possible, but eventually it was impossible to prevent people from finding out that he was deaf. He gradually became more private, and eventually gave most of his time to composing rather than performing.

As he lay on his deathbed, one of his last acts was to take communion. Interestingly, his death came during a loud and violent storm, and possibly this is a reflection of the internal life he had led. Although he led a life of turmoil, he was passionate about his relationship with God, even though Beethoven's faith was unorthodox. He was very private about his beliefs, and had an interest in other religions. It has been said that he copied three Hindu passages that he hid under a glass in his desk.

It is clear from private letters and books that he tried to seek out God to find solace and meaning for his life. He was also a generous man, helping his friends any way he could by giving his money and talents when it was needed to help others. Even though some aspects of his personality and life seemed to contradict his faith, he was a man who was tormented inside and desperate to experience God.

In a letter to a friend, he wrote: "I have no friend. I must live by myself. I know, however, that God is nearer to me than others. I go without fear to Him, I have constantly recognized and understood Him."

Charles and John Wesley

Charles Wesley (1707–1788) and John Wesley (1703–1791) broke denominational boundaries with their music.[164] In 1738, on a missions trip to Georgia, they had an authentic conversion experience. Greatly influenced by Moravian believers, known for their powerful hymn singing and emphasis on worship through music, John translated a number of their hymns into German. Charles was a great preacher, yet it was his astounding talent for writing hymns that captured the essence of faith in Christ. In his hymns, of which he wrote more than 6500, he had a gift for capturing the praises of the human spirit. Even though the Wesleys had not formally studied music, their work displayed a magnificent connection between musical structure and lyrics. Interestingly, in the late 1740s, Handel wrote three melodies for Charles Wesley's lyrics: *Sinners*, *Obey the Gospel Word*, *O Love Divine*, and *Rejoice, the Lord is King*.

The Wesley brothers' passion was to write hymns that everyone could sing. Historically, music within the church was scripture sung to music, often taken from the Psalms and there was a separation between choir and congregation, or part-singing. The works of the Wesley brothers enabled the congregation to enter into worship while integrating with the spirit of their inspiring music.

20

Realism collides with Romanticism

I dream my painting, and then I paint my dream.[165]
Vincent Van Gogh

*I did not compose my work as one might put on a
church vestment ... rather it sprung from the truly
fervent faith of my heart, such as I have felt it since
my childhood.*[166] Franz Liszt

19th century

The mid-1700s to the early 1800s was known as the Realism
period. This was a time where artists strove to paint exactly what
they saw, rather than idealizing or romanticizing.

The late 1700 to the mid-1800s was known as the Romantic period, an era where the arts flourished and great artists were highly respected for their genius. Often revered as being "above human," some artists during this age were egotistical and often immoral. Instead of frowning upon these character flaws, the public usually admired and celebrated them, as if they lived beyond all human rules. Many artists were imaginative, expressed a desire for greater freedom, and were passionate and rebellious. Richard Wagner, the great composer (who was also an anti-Semite), is an example of one man who was highly revered as "super-human" for his talents. More than 10,000 biographies were written about him before his death!

Art

In 1867 until about 1886, the visual arts were marked by what we call Impressionism, an art style that promoted matter and form over subject. French artists such as Claude Monet (1840–1926) led this new movement in painting, and other Impressionists included Renoir and Degas. The musical arts were soon to follow this theme, and the era produced some of the greatest musical talents of all time: composers such as Franz Liszt (1811–85), not only a composer but a trained priest; Richard Wagner (1813–1883); Giuseppe Verdi (1813–1901); Johannes Brahms (1833–1897); Ludwig van Beethoven (circa 1770–1827); Frederic Chopin (1810–1849); and Peter Tchaikovsky (1840–1893).

Vincent van Gogh (1853–1890)

Vincent van Gogh, a post-Impressionist, was one of the leaders in Expressionism. Even today, he remains one of the world's most popular artists and his work is among the most expensive to buy. He famously suffered from reoccurring mental illness, and during one episode, he cut off his left ear. Although he started a career in painting late in his life, he produced about 2000 works (1100 drawings and 900 paintings) in the last ten years of his life, and created his best-known works in the last two years of his life. Yet this great man, whom we hold in such high esteem today, only ever sold one painting in his lifetime.

Ministry

It is during this period that we begin to see a strong separation between the "sacred and the secular." People began to view the spiritual world—prayer, worship, scriptures—and the material world as completely separate entities. This caused a decline in church attendances.

D.L. Moody

In the late 1800s, the great preacher Dwight L. Moody teamed up with soloist and song leader Ira D. Sankey to lead crusades in what is called the American Evangelical Movement. Their influence in Europe, predominately in England, made a great impact for spreading the Gospel. They published a pamphlet of songs entitled *Sacred Songs and Solos*, which was continually expanded and updated. By 1903, there were more than 1200 items contained in it. The idea of a preacher and guest musician/worship leader is still a popular way to minister today.

The Salvation Army

Founded by William Booth (1829–1912), the "Salvos" have done much for nations around the world. The international movement, even today, combines a quasi-military structure with evangelical, social and charitable work. Their message is to spread the Gospel to all who would hear, without preference. Booth's methods were unconventional and led to friction with the traditional framework of the church. Eventually he went out on his own to take the Gospel to the people, against the wishes of the leaders of the church in London (and aren't we glad he did!). In time, because of his success in converting so many people to Christ, he was considered a great leader in Britain. Between 1881 and 1885 alone, The Salvation Army converted more than 250,000 to Christianity.

Literary

A number of famous authors made their mark during the 19th century. In England, among the most popular were Charles Dickens, Jane Austen and the poet John Keats. In Russia, probably the finest authors were Leo Tolstoy, Fyodor Dostoevsky and Anton Chekhov. Oscar Wilde, born in Ireland, was a brilliant but controversial figure and Mark Twain and Edgar Allan Poe were among the leading America writers. Robert Louis Stevenson (1850–1894), the Scottish novelist, wrote *Treasure Island*, and *The Strange Case of Dr. Jekyll and Mr. Hyde*.

Music

Black gospel

By the end of the 19th century, other forms of music were beginning to emerge into wider audiences.[167] Negro spirituals—which had its roots in African music—black gospel (both were initially considered the music of the slaves), white gospel music, and white southern gospel began to reach a wider audience. This type of music is highly emotive; whether its songs are about hardship or joy, it is easy to be caught up in its spirit.

In early colonial times in America, accompanied music in the church was not common. English migrants brought with them a limited knowledge of about eight songs that mainly consisted of the Psalms they had sung in their homeland. They brought few instruments with them (cargo space was too limited to waste on musical equipment). There were no songbooks and no instruments in their early pilgrim church services. As a result, they would perform what was called "lining," where the leader would sing one line, and then the congregation would repeat it.

To these puritans, music and the arts as a form of pleasure was not acceptable. There was much controversy about how people should sing songs in church, or if they should even sing at all. Some puritans felt that singing should only be allowed for Christians and that heathen Indians should have only the privilege of saying "amen" at the end of a song. Other puritan groups felt that women should not be allowed to sing, while some even felt that if a song was not spiritual in nature it should not be sung at all.

With the birth of the triangular slave trade in America, Negros captured from Africa brought their soulful spiritual music into the sparse and desolate landscape of this musical Christian history. The emergence of their sound came from great oppression as the slave trade began to thrive. There was such a demand for slaves that some traders were expected to bring back around 3000 per year to remain in standing with the British Government. Some tribal leaders in Africa were provoking wars between tribes, as it was acceptable to sell their enemies to the new Americans. Some slaves were traded for metals and other materials.

During this time, Africans would use their musical instruments during wars against their enemies. Many African tribes did not use words in their music at all, but just rhythms and chants. They would beat their drums and chant songs incanting their gods to bring storms against the English ships that were coming to capture them. They believed the power of music could bring destruction against their enemies and keep them safe.

It is easy to imagine that when these slaves were brought back to America their sound was unacceptable to the pilgrims and the puritans. However, some slave owners found their music entertaining. This was a sound they had never heard before and they enjoyed hearing this new musical form. Within the church, there were no choirs because music was not an important part of early colonial life—there was a country and community to build! The new sound the Negros were bringing was unique and inspiring.

Many white plantation owners enjoyed their singing so

much that they would allow the slaves to sing whilst they worked in the fields, although they were not allowed to speak. Imagine the sound coming from the fields as the slaves worked in the hot sun. One person would set up a tempo and they would begin to sing as they worked in the cotton fields.

Most of these slaves remained uneducated. They could not read and so the way they would learn scripture was to sing it. This is how they began to remember the scriptures and, without realizing it, they were aligning themselves with the Word of God as they sang. Without understanding what they were doing, they would prophetically sing of being free and having release. As they were serving the "white man" they sang of their own freedom. They were actually prophesying their future. Their owners had no idea what they were doing, only that they enjoyed the sounds that were coming from the fields.

Eventually, many slave owners befriended their slaves and began to love them. They began to bring them to church, and suddenly black people were being saved and black churches began to spring up all over America, especially in Kentucky where there was less oppression. A great revival occurred, yet as the slave owners began to see the strength rising within their slaves, some brought harsher oppression upon them as they were afraid of what may happen if their power grew.

The Negros brought with them their superstitions from Africa and applied them to their newfound faith. There were two main types of music for which they were known. One was the "spiritual." This was where the singer would sit on a chair and rock back and forth and their whole body, soul and spirit would feel the emotion of what they were singing. The second was the "shout." This was very much a call and response. One person would have a stick and the "stick man" would beat out a rhythm on the floor. People would clap and stomp their feet to the rhythm. As they shuffled around a room, someone would read a scripture aloud and the rest would repeat that line. They shuffled their feet because they believed that if their feet left the ground they would trip over the cross and go to Hell. Yet even among all their superstitious beliefs, God heard their cry and was able to bring freedom and understanding of His love for them.

21

Science and the computer age

In the future everyone will be famous for 15 minutes.[168]
Andy Warhol

I believe in Christianity as I believe that the sun has risen not only because I see it, but because by it I see everything else.[169] C.S. Lewis

20th century

The 20th century saw incredible scientific and technological advances, greater than ever before. The motor car was invented, man walked on the moon, but weapons of incredibly destructive power were created.

At the end of the 19th century, it was a commonly held view that almost everything in terms of scientific discovery was known, but with advancements in the field of quantum physics and the development of the theory of relativity, came the realization that the Universe was far less fathomable than had previously been imagined.

The 20th century was also marked by the dawn of the computer age. The first computer invented was as large as a room in a house. Invented in the 1940s, it was used to solve difficult mathematical equations. By the 1980s the Internet was accessible.

At the beginning of the century, Paris was the central hub for writers, musicians, painters and other artists. However, by the end of the 20th century it was America—predominately New York and Los Angeles—that became the focus for culture and the arts. Music, film and other media influenced fashion and culture, and of course, with most movies coming out of America, American culture began to take a foothold in other parts of the world.

Literature

A list of great 20th century authors and their works would fill many pages. The following are just some of the most popular writers of that era who have left an indelible mark on history with their work:[170]

> J.R.R. Tolkien (*The Hobbit, Lord of the Rings*), C.S. Lewis (*The Lion, the Witch and the Wardrobe*), George Orwell (*1984* and *Animal Farm*), Harper Lee (*To Kill a Mockingbird*), John Steinbeck (*The Grapes of Wrath*), F. Scott Fitzgerald (*The Great Gatsby*), William Golding (*Lord of the Flies*), Kenneth Grahame (*Wind in the Willows*) and Margaret Mitchell (*Gone with the Wind*).

Musical styles

Music and musical art forms grew considerably in the 20th century, mainly due to rapid changes in technology. The radio allowed people from all over the world to hear many different musical styles, which created worldwide fame for some performers. Music videos were produced, and this led to copyright laws being strengthened, although with new technology it also became much easier to illegally produce music products. Electronic instruments such as the synthesizer were invented, which brought a new sound and much experimentation.

In 1948, the first 12-inch 33½ rpm vinyl LP record was introduced by Columbia Records. By 1964, the first audio cassette recorder was introduced in the USA. In 1982, the first compact discs went on sale in Europe and Japan. In 1988, CDs sold more than LPs for the first time.

Pop music

More than any other era, pop artists have had a profound cultural influence worldwide. Here are just some of the popular artists who have affected music and culture in the 20th century:

> Elvis Presley, Stevie Wonder, Ray Charles, James Brown, Little Richard, Bob Marley, Otis Redding, BB King, Buddy Holly, Billy Holiday, Roy Orbison, George Gershwin, Willie Nelson, Eric Clapton, Elton John, Billy Joel, John Cougar Mellencamp, Johnny Cash, Janis Joplin, Prince, Madonna, Bob Dylan, Simon and Garfunkel, Van Morrison, Joni Mitchell, Bruce Springsteen, Jimi Hendrix and Carole King. The list is endless!

Many bands have attained incredible popularity in all corners of the globe:

> The Rolling Stones, The Beatles, The Who, Led Zeppelin, The Eagles, REM, Pink Floyd, Fleetwood Mac, The Police, The Doors, The Beach Boys, and U2 are among the most famous.

Pop Art

Pop Art became one of the largest art movements in the 20th century. The emergence of Pop Art began in the 1950s in Britain, but originated in a somewhat different form in the USA, and eventually spread to other parts of the world. Pop Art focused on using modern images such as comic books and advertising to create art that reached a broad range of people, until the art form itself became part of popular culture.

Andy Warhol

One of the leading figures in the Pop Art Movement was Andy Warhol (1928–1987). An American filmmaker and painter, he was an incredibly creative and eccentric man. Having been a successful commercial illustrator early on in his career, he was also a record producer, author, and public figure who was well known in elitist social circles. His paintings of a Campbell's Soup can and a Coca Cola can are two of his most recognizable works. He is also well known for painting celebrities such as Marilyn Monroe.

His movies and other works were often sexually explicit, and he was one of the first men to openly admit to being gay. However, he was also incredibly religious. A Byzantine Rite Catholic, he went to church almost every day, and often volunteered to help in homeless shelters in New York. Many of the works that he created later in his life had hidden religious themes.

Bob Dylan

Arguably, one of the most influential figures of this era was Bob Dylan.[171] Born Robert Allan Zimmerman on May 24, 1941 in Minnesota USA into a Jewish family, Bob Dylan became the voice of a disillusioned generation. Even though he has shunned the label of prophet and role model, his songs gave people a voice and made them think for themselves.

Dylan had a way of writing lyrics that captured the spirit of the era and the heart of the people. He had a way of connecting with people through his songs. Gospel songs such as *Gotta Serve Somebody*, or his more well-known songs such as *Like a Rolling Stone, The Times They Are a-Changing, Blowin' in the Wind* and *Hurricane* still hit home and stand the test of time.

Dylan was considered a spearhead for a new era of artistic culture. Bruce Springsteen once said of him: "Bob freed the mind the way Elvis freed the body . . . He invented a new way a pop singer could sound, broke through the limitations of what a recording artist could achieve, and changed the face of rock and roll forever."[172]

As with most artists who were leading the way, he was often misunderstood and criticized. Folk music was predominately known for its acoustic feel. When Dylan introduced the electric guitar to his music, it was met with a mostly negative reaction. His hardcore folk fans did not like the change at all. Some people thought he had sold out. This is hard to imagine today where a majority of popular music is guitar driven.

In 1979, it was speculated that he had converted to Christianity. He had always used biblical references in his music, but there was evidence to suggest that he had truly become a Christian. After his apparent conversion took place he began to write more overtly spiritual songs, but he often denied publicly that he had converted. Christian bookstores refused to sell his albums, unconvinced by his new spiritual convictions. Yet he has been called a prophet of our time. And like a prophet, was often criticized and misunderstood. On his Still on the Road Second Gospel Tour in 1980, he said from the stage: "Years ago they . . . said I was a prophet. I used to say, 'No I'm not a prophet' . . . they say: 'Yes you are, you are a prophet.' I said, 'No it is not me.' They used to say: 'You sure are a prophet.' They used to convince me I was a prophet. Now I come out and say Jesus Christ is the answer. They say, 'Bob Dylan's no prophet.' They just can't handle it."[173]

His music influenced other predominant artists of his time, and even though he has left his mark in his own generation, he continues to engage new fans with every decade. Dylan is someone who is still as relevant today as he was when he first began his career.

22

The emergence of a Christian music industry (CCM)

Art is more engaging than propaganda.[174] Larry Norman
Life is God's art.[175] Larry Norman

The "Jesus Movement" and music

Beginning in the late '60s on the West Coast of the USA, the Jesus Movement emerged as a counterculture among the hippie generation.[176] Dissatisfied with a society that allowed the Vietnam War, and spurred on by peace, drugs and "free love," the hippie generation was born, and out of the hippie culture emerged what became known as the "Jesus freak" or "Jesus people." Young people were beginning to testify to authentic encounters with a personable God, with signs, wonders and healings following.

Unlike many other revival movements, there was not one person at the helm leading the way. Many different people lent their influences to the Jesus Movement. People such as Rev. Duane Pederson, who coined the phrases "Jesus people" and "Jesus Movement," published the Hollywood Free Paper, an evangelistic tool that represented the underground, but emerging, movement of the "Jesus people."

Chuck Smith of Calvary Chapel and Lonnie Frisbee ministered to the counter-culture, and reached people on the streets. Today under Chuck Smith's leadership, Calvary Chapel has grown across the world to be one of the largest denominations to exist in the last 50 years. Other significant figures include Arthur Blessitt, minister of the Sunset Strip and founder of His Place nightclub, and Greg Laurie who is still considered "the evangelist of the MTV generation." Others included Ted Wise, one of the first people to be converted to Christianity through the Movement, and Linda Meissner who had a vision of thousands of young people marching for Jesus and founded the Jesus People Army. Jim Palosaari, who founded Servant's Highway ministries and JPUSA in Britain, is also one of the founders of Greenbelt Festival, one of the largest Christian music festivals in the world. These are but a few of the people who made a huge impact through the Jesus Movement.

A focus of the Jesus Movement was ministry in coffee houses and on the streets, the premise being to meet people where they lived. This resulted in a huge evangelistic outreach that saw many people saved who were dissatisfied with the status quo. It is no surprise that this counter-culture birthed what was coined "Jesus music," which became the foundation for what we now know today as the Contemporary Christian Music industry.

Artists and bands such as Larry Norman (*I Wish We'd all Been Ready*), Randy Stonehill, Glen Kaiser and the Resurrection band (Glen is still a pastor of a Jesus Movement church today), Petra, 2nd Chapter of Acts, Phil Keaggy, Andrea Crouch and the Disciples, Mark Heard, Sweet Comfort Band, Daniel Amos, and later Keith Green, all paved the way.

Jesus communities/commenes and coffee houses began to crop up throughout the USA. In 1971, *Time* magazine named Jesus Christ as their man of the year. As Jesus music began to multiply in influence, the mainstream media took interest and its own industry began to emerge.

Radio stations solely devoted to Christian music began to grow, as did magazines, festivals and concerts. Many record companies snatched up Christian artists because of their huge fan bases. However, there were also many who refused to sign with these companies, feeling that they would be selling out and that their message would be compromised. They were not interested in becoming money-making machines, and did not want to convolute the message of the Gospel with public relations-driven practices. Thus, the foundations were put in place for the Christian music industry, one of the fastest growing mediums in music today.

Nevertheless, Jesus Music was not without its attacks from church circles. Many felt that marrying rock 'n' roll with Christian lyrics was not representative of true Christian faith. Most Christian artists were thought to have "sold out" to popular culture. Yet as church membership in traditional denominations began to decline, evangelical churches began to grow at a fast rate. Between 1967 and 1972, around 800 Jesus communal houses were established, and the Hollywood Free Paper was averaging around 200,000 copies per issue.

Larry Norman

In 1969, the first Christian rock album was released by the man considered to be the father of Christian rock—Larry Norman.[177] Larry was the first person to combine the flavours of rock music with Gospel lyrics. The album titled *Upon this Rock* featured the infamous song *I Wish We'd all Been Ready*. *Time* magazine called him "the most important writer since Paul Simon."

Norman's career began in 1966 when he signed to Capitol Records, the same label that released The Beatles and The Beach Boys. He had strong opinions about his faith and expressed them openly, both through his music and his concerts. Larry and his band found themselves opening for artists such as The Grateful Dead, Janis Joplin and The Doors, among many others.

Even though *Upon this Rock* was thought to be the first Christian rock album, Larry had been performing and recording for years before the Jesus Movement made contemporary Christian music popular. In fact, according to his website, his musical style courted controversy for about 15 years before the Jesus Movement was even born. During the Jesus Movement era, the church was wary of Larry Norman and his new musical style. *Upon this Rock* was banned from most Christian bookstores for more than two years, and his next album *Only Visiting this Planet* was held in limbo for more than six years. Secular record stores readily had his albums available, whereas Christian music outlets often did not. Even though the church rejected this modern day prophet, his music resonated with a youth culture that was desperate for an authentic experience of Christ through music.

In 1974, after leaving MGM records, he started his own record label—Solid Rock Records. However, his albums were still regarded as too controversial for widespread release. These albums included *Orphans of Eden*, as well as *In Another Land* (which was censored by Word records) and *Something New under the Son*.

According to his website, Larry also discovered the relatively obscure Randy Stonehill, helped him off drugs, produced the album *Welcome to Paradise* and took him on tour. He also discovered Steve Camp, Daniel Amos, Mark Heard, Scott Wesley Brown, Steve Taylor, and it is possible that he even nurtured a young Keith Green.

Larry was an artist who was ahead of his time. Even though

he had always been on the cutting edge of music experimentation, he never was completely understood by the industry. However, his heart was always for the people and in the early 1980s he found that through mail order he could sell directly to the public and shun the distributors who had always shunned him.

His music is as influential today as it was decades ago. Artists such as DC Talk, Rebecca St. James and Audio Adrenaline have recorded his songs, and a new generation has connected with his music. This was evident in 2001 when he was inducted into the Gospel Music Hall of Fame. Even though he suffered many setbacks in his final years—including a plane crash, a heart attack and major surgery—he continued to tour and record albums until his death in February 2008. He wrote songs that challenged common mindsets within the Christian faith, which made him popular with a generation that wanted to change the status quo, yet others were wary of his outspokenness. It is this paradox that made him an artist who stood out from the rest:

> "I want the people to know that He saved my soul
> But I still like to listen to the radio
> They say rock 'n' roll is wrong we'll give you one more chance
> I say I feel so good I gotta get up and dance
> I know what's right, I know what's wrong, I do not confuse it,
> Why should the devil have all the good music?"[178]

The emergence of a Christian music industry

With the rapid advances in technology came more diversity in art, culture and music. As more artists displayed a deep conviction of faith, Christian music began to pave its own way and expand into its own industry. In the 1970s, new labels and orchestration included Jimmy Owens, Rick Powell, Paul Johnson, Otis Skillings, Bob Krogstad, Buryl Red and Ronn Huff.

23

Contemporary Christian music and the rebirth of church worship

A song is anything that can walk by itself.[179] Bob Dylan

The Charismatic Movement and worship

The Charismatic Movement affected a change in worship styles in a dramatic way.[180] By the early 1970s a true renewal, with an emphasis on the Holy Spirit, brought new life into churches across America and Britain. As a result of the influence of the hippy culture and the Jesus Movement, the focus was on love and this brought new freedom into the Charismatic churches. The way worship was expressed underwent considerable change. Creative gifts—in particular, dance, poetry and music—were encouraged from within congregations, which meant both the church and the arts thrived. There was a sense of love for God and for the people at the essence of this new surge of creativity.

Music within the Charismatic Movement was much more commercial than music featured in traditional worship. It compared in quality and style to what was happening in the "real world," which made it more accessible to the younger generation. Interestingly, as this movement grew, its songs also embraced a broader range of topics than songs in traditional worship. Instead of just singing about joy, peace and love, songs were written that featured many different emotions. The Iona Community, from the Island of Iona just off the north-west coast of Scotland was one of the communities that embraced these new ideals. Although steeped in biblical theology, themes were embraced that were unacceptable in the past. Loss, sorrow and frustration are some of the themes expressed in hymns such as *When Grief is Raw*, *Stumbling Blocks* and *Stepping Stones*.

The significant difference in musical forms between the Charismatic Movement and church movements in the past was that the Charismatic musical style happened from within the church itself. The frustrated artist who loved God often could not find their place to create great works of art within the old church framework. In the new movement, however, people freely expressed what was happening within a community of believers. It is interesting to note that the Charismatic Movement was not widely accepted within the majority of church circles, yet its influence within the arts is evident even today.

Other significant events within Christian music

In 1979, Bob Dylan's *Slow Train Coming* gospel album was released.[181] In 1982, Amy Grant's *Age to Age* became the first gold album on a gospel label by a solo artist. In 1984, Stryper's *Yellow and Black Attack* became the first Christian metal album ever released. In 1985, Amy Grant had the first CCM crossover hit with *Find a Way*. Then in 1991 and 1992, Amy Grant (*That's What Love is For*, and *Baby Baby*), Kathy Troccoli (*Everything*

Changes) and Michael W. Smith (*I Will be Here for You*) had hits outside of the Christian music scene. In December 1999, Cliff Richard's *Millennium Prayer*, which combined the words of the *Lord's Prayer* with the melody of *Auld Lang Syne*, became the UK's number one single in sales for three weeks, despite being rejected for airplay by many British radio stations.

Since then, its been almost commonplace to see Christian artists crossing over into mainstream music, or artists with a deep Christian faith expressing songs of faith within the mainstream music framework.[182] Bands such as Switchfoot, Jars of Clay, MXPX, Mute Math, and of course U2, are examples of this. Seattle-based Tooth and Nail Records have uncovered bands such as Under Oath and The Almost on their label. Worship bands Hillsong and Hillsong United have also had success on the mainstream Australian charts. CCM artist Bob Carlisle had a number one hit song with *Butterfly Kisses* in the USA, Mercy Me and their moving song *I Can Only Imagine*, with its overtly Christian lyrics, reached the top five in the USA. Other artists who have influenced the mainstream from the CCM platform include Mark Shultz, Chris Rice and Mary Mary.

Other well-known artists who are not part of the CCM scene but are Christians who work within the mainstream industry, include Natasha and Daniel Beddingfield in the UK, Australian Idol winner Guy Sebastian, and New Zealand's Brooke Fraser. Other American bands and artists who have a faith in God include Lifehouse (who were actually worship leaders), The Fray and Lauryn Hill. Probably one of the most important popular music figures to express their Christian faith over the last 30 years is Irish lead singer Bono from U2. Other artists who have expressed some sort of faith are Creed (especially lead singer Scott Stapp), POD, Chevele, Evanescence, Justin Timberlake, Prince, Beyonce, OutKast, and Michelle Williams.

Many who have had mainstream success, whether from the

CCM industry or directly within the secular music industry, are not often widely accepted or praised by the church at large. Unfortunately, most churches find their faith questionable. Maybe this is because sometimes their actions do not portray what mainstream church culture would promote as Christian conduct. Whether this is true or not, it is interesting that over the centuries many artists who had some sort of faith in God have experienced the same controversy within the church, yet it is their art that goes beyond the church to influence a wide audience.

Humanity is complex and diverse, and if we try to compartmentalize people we will never be satisfied when they break the mold of our expectations. People will always make mistakes, and as true Christians we should endeavour to embrace each other and work through our misunderstandings rather than dismiss and judge. There is no more effective way to crush the creative spirit than when we do this, especially in the name of God.

Worship music

Worship music—that is, music specifically written for congregations to sing—has grown significantly over the years. This has allowed people from many denominations around the world to sing songs of praise and love to the Lord in fresh ways. The worship genre is quite broad, from prophetic worship artists such as Kevin Prosch and Jason Upton, to the more pop/mainstream sounds of Delirious, Matt Redman, Chris Tomlin, Tim Hughes, Brenton Brown, Darlene Zschech and the Hillsong team, and to the more traditional styles of Graham Kendrick and the Celtic sounds of Robin Mark.

Today, worship music is currently considered by many to be the fastest growing and predominant form of Christian music. It has allowed churches worldwide to worship with one voice, capturing the spirit of nations and the heart of God. Songs such as *Shout to the Lord* (Darlene Zschech),[183] *Here I am to Worship* (Tim Hughes) and *How Great is Our God* (made famous by Chris Tomlin) are powerful songs sung by millions, and in essence help us as one church become unified in our worship of God, and in interceding for the Earth.

24

The arts today and passion for the supernatural

In Europe AD 1000 the popular heroes were soldiers and saints. In AD 2000 they were more likely, in many parts of the world, to be athletes, actors, singers, artists or other heroes of leisure time.[184] Geoffrey Blainey

Sport and leisure

*T*oday, a major focus of modern life revolves around leisure, entertainment and lifestyle. Sports and popular entertainment are the priorities. Plasma TV screens, DVD players, iPods and the Wii or X-Box can be found in most family homes.

Sport has become a religion in itself. England and Australia were two of the first countries to lead the way with spectator sport. Originally, sport was not played on Sunday because the Sabbath was respected as a day of rest, whether people were religious or not.

The increase in powerful floodlighting meant that sporting events could be played at night, and now sporting contests are likely to take place on every day of the week. These days, the exuberance of a sports fan on a Sunday is much more common than a person reflecting their passion worshipping God in a church service!

Population growth

The world's population has grown significantly in the past 50 years. At the time of Christ, it was estimated at around 300 million, which is currently around the population size of the United States. By 1750, it is estimated that there were around 800 million people on Earth, which is less than the current population of China. A huge increase happened around 1800 when the world's population grew to an estimated one billion. This doubled in the next 125 years. Between 1927 and 1974, it doubled again to about 4 billion people. From 1974–1999 the world's population increased by another 2 billion people.

It's hard to believe that in the 1990s alone more people were added to the population than at any other time in history. The main reason for this is the advance in fertility treatments, which has naturally led to an increase in birth rates.

Where is the connection to art in this? New discoveries in technology have meant that many art forms are now electronically accessible in most countries in the world. These advances mean that art has the power to influence communities and even nations; as the world's population increases, the influence of art increases exponentially. Today, something can be created and uploaded onto the Internet and viewed around the world on the same day that it was created. Astounding!

Global warming and terrorism

Today, the two most prominent threats to humankind come from natural disasters and terrorism.

Thirty years ago, the view that the world was becoming warmer due to a hole in the ozone layer was of minor concern and was not widely discussed. Now this is one of the most important topics of discussion in every nation.

There is an unpredictability in nature, and tsunamis, earthquakes, floods and cyclones have occurred in various places in the world, with tragic consequences. The threat of terrorism is also a worldwide problem.

Now, the very science and technology that was praised in earlier centuries is often considered a curse. Environmental concerns, such as pollution and global warming, are deemed to have occurred as a result of rampant technological and scientific advancements. We are bonded in our fight to rid the world of terrorist acts, and to see our planet sustainable and healthy. Our concerns are certainly reflected throughout the medium of the arts.

Religion and science

Religion was often the backbone of society in the early centuries. Helpless to control nature, societies often appealed to the gods to provide health for their families and good harvests for their crops. Often Kings or Emperors ordered people to follow a certain religion and those that did not were punished by death. Consequently, almost everyone believed in a god or the imposed religion just to stay alive.

In the 20th century came greater affluence, a better quality of life, longer life spans and scientific and technological advancements, and as a result the need for God reduced significantly and church attendances declined. This was most evident after the World War II.

However, faith was still alive, and churches that refused to follow popular trends and stuck to what they firmly believed regardless of the culture of the day were the ones that thrived in troubled times. I think this is still true today.

Within the Christian churches today, it is the Pentecostal denominations that see the largest growth worldwide: "With more than 580 million adherents (growing by 19 million per year and 54,000 per day), the Pentecostal/Charismatic Movement has become, in just 100 years, the fastest growing and most globally diverse expression of worldwide Christianity. At the current rate of growth, some researchers predict there will be 1 billion Pentecostals by 2025, most located in Asia, Africa, and Latin America."[185]

We are beginning to see a revival throughout the Christian church. This is evident in church attendances, and the increase of the supernatural with healings and visions. Music and entertainment is wrought with supernatural and religious themes. People are looking for something that is greater than themselves. Factors that influence church growth could be concerns about the environment and the threat of terrorism, as more people look for a way to receive comfort and hope in a troubled world.

Movies/media/books

In the last 10 to 15 years, there has been a growth in supernatural, religious and spiritual themes in books and electronic media. Shows such as *Touched by an Angel*, *Crossing Over with John Edward*, *Medium*, *The Ghost Whisperer*, *The X-files*, *Supernatural* and even *The Simpsons*, have explored topics of a spiritual nature. Books such as *The Da Vinci Code*, *The Secret* and the *Harry Potter* series have a spiritual side to them. The popularity of movies such as *Butterfly Effect*, *Sixth Sense*, *Lady in the Water*, *The Da Vinci Code*, *The Passion of the Christ*, *Lord of the Rings* and *The Chronicles of Narnia* (to name a few), could indicate a deep desire to discover something beyond that which we see.

It seems that people are hungry for more of a spiritual connection, and I believe it's because, in the absence of a true and experiential relationship with God, people search for other spiritual means to fill their sense that something is missing. To be created in the image of God means that we also have a spirit—like God who is spirit. When there is an absence of God in our lives, it is our spirit that is unfulfilled. People are beginning to fill this void with movies and books that have spiritual themes. The rise in the exploration of more of a spiritual connection is because people need God, although at times they are looking for Him in the wrong places. The more we turn away from God, the more emptiness we feel and the more we search for truth. The truth we seek can only be found in Christ. I am saddened to say that many so-called Christians are influenced by these themes because they are not experiencing God in a real and authentic way. We attend church and go through the motions, but we do not experience His presence in the way we should.

Music

Throughout the ages, spirituality has always been an important topic in music, and the current era is no exception. In the 1960s, with artists such as Bob Dylan, along with the hippie culture and Jesus Movements, we began to see a focus on spirituality across popular music genres. Music that explores these themes is still pertinent today and is growing stronger each year.

It is common for artists who are not in the Christian music industry to have overtly spiritual themes throughout their music. In fact, some secular artists seem to have more obvious Christian lyrics than most CCM artists. The spectrum of emotions from fans and music industries is widespread. Some people become confused when an artist's lifestyle or shows represent something different from what they perceive as a genuine faith. Others can become frustrated or angry that personal spiritual opinions overshadow the "entertainment" of art.

Added frustrations have come from the Christian Music

industry itself, labelling artists outside of the CCM industry with some sort of spiritual banner, yet being unable to connect with them because of perceived contradictions. These artists often do not seem to fit the mold, yet at the same time they influence many people with their beliefs. Examples of bands in this category would be U2, Creed, and Evanescence.

U2 are one band that has undoubtedly mastered expression of their faith in a way most people can understand. Bono's spiritual outlook is undeniably God-focused. Lyrics from the song *I Still Haven't Found What I'm Looking For*, from *The Joshua Tree* album, are overtly spiritual:

> "I have spoke with the tongues of angels" and "You broke the bonds/You loosed the chains/You carried the cross/And my shame/And my shame/You know I believe it."

Bono once said: "I love to think that music can be an instrument of grace, that there might be mercy in melody and that at the very least a great song can fill the silence of indifference we sometimes find in our hearts."[186]

Lenny Kravitz, on his *Circus* album expresses his views in the song *The Resurrection*:

> "If you could feel what I could feel/Well then you'd know His love is real/If you could hear what I could hear/Well then you'd know the King is near."

At times, Kravitz confuses his audience by mixing Bible-based theology with sexual references. To add to the confusion there have been several stories about his many infidelities during his marriage to Lisa Bonet, although never publicly confirmed. Regardless, it is obvious by reading his lyrics that he is searching for answers and has a relationship with God. He once said: "God is always in my life and that is the most important thing to me."[187]

Scott Stapp, from the band Creed, has also written lyrics that reflect a longing for the spiritual. In his song *Unforgiven* he encourages his listeners to:

"Step inside the light and see the fear of God burn inside of me . . . The gold was put to flame/To kill, to burn, to mold its purity."

In the song *My Own Prison*:

"I hear a thunder in the distance/See a vision of a cross/I feel the pain that was given/On that sad day of loss." Two years after the song was released, Stapp admitted in an interview, "The message of salvation is in 'My Own Prison' and I did not think about it until after it was done."

How engaging that God is at work in the artist's life without them even realizing it!

The band Creed were mixing their album *Weathered* during the fateful attacks on New York on 11 September 2001. The songs, all written before the attacks, were incredibly timely and relevant to the world. Songs such as *Bullets*, *Who's got my back* and *Signs* are examples of these. The song *Freedom Fighter* has lyrics that all their fans could relate to during this time: "I'm just a freedom fighter, no remorse . . . raging on in holy war."[188]

25

What we can learn from the past

Life is God's novel. Let him write it.[189] Isaac Bashevis Singer

The diversity of temporality is painfully at odds with the oneness of the everlasting, as is its ontological lack and deficiency in comparison with the fullness of divine being.[190] Jeremy S. Begbie

After reading the last few chapters, you may have already come to your own conclusions on what we can learn from the past. Maybe you have been challenged and encouraged; maybe you now have a greater understanding about why we find ourselves in the state we are in. My hope is that you can move forward with confidence into the future, making new paths that are strong and influential. I hope you avoid the pitfalls that our brothers and sisters have encountered. May we all learn from their mistakes yet build on the legacy they have left behind.

This passage says it so well:

1 Cor 10:1 *These are all warning markers—danger!—*
in our history books, written down so that we do not
repeat their mistakes. Our positions in the story are
parallel—they at the beginning, we at the end—and
we are just as capable of messing it up as they were.

The arts are supernatural gifts

The arts are as ancient as the world and music was evident at the dawn of creation, even before the worlds began.

Job 38:4 *Where were you when I laid the Earth's*
foundation? . . . Who laid its cornerstone?—while the
morning stars sang together and all the angels shouted
for joy?[191]

The stars were singing when God laid the Earth's foundation. Can you imagine the scene as God flings stars into space with his mighty hand? A symphony is heard throughout the Universe, as the mass angel choir joins in with joyous praise. It is a moving image. NASA has even recorded some of the sounds the planets, stars and the earth make—space is certainly not a silent blackness, but a song waiting to be heard by those who will listen.

If it is true that music was here before the Earth was made, then it could be possible that creativity is not an earthly gift but a heavenly one; a supernatural medium that manifests itself when we are creative. We are tapping into the supernatural world, going beyond that which we see to bring the reality of Heaven to a world that has become numb to the ways of the spirit. The sound of Heaven is waiting for human ears and lips to become carriers of the presence of the Kingdom; in this realm, creativity is dripping like honey, available to all who are willing to taste it.

It is no surprise that art has had a tremendous influence on culture. History has proven that it certainly is a powerful medium. In fact, it has been said that if someone wants to destroy a nation, they only need to destroy its art and it will crumble. If you study the history of war, you will notice that when armies infiltrated communities they burnt the books of the vanquished, destroyed their museums and art galleries, pulled down their statues and grand buildings. Taking away art means taking away heritage and history. When that is gone, there is little left.

History is filled with many examples of this. In 1988, author Salman Rushdie had a death sentence or "fatwah" placed on him by fundamentalist Iranian leaders. His novel *The Satanic Verses* was considered blasphemous by Islamic groups. He went into hiding for several years, and although unharmed to this day, several other people who worked on the book have been killed or have survived assassination attempts.[192]

When The Beatles became popular, Russian youth did whatever they could to get their hands on their music, which was illegal to purchase at the time. Albums were smuggled into Russia printed on the plates of X-rays. Years later, discussing Paul McCartney's first trip to Moscow on Larry King Live, author Richard Shenkman said: ". . . if you've got 100 historians in a room and you ask them for three days what were the causes of the break up of the Soviet Union, I'm sure that probably not one of them would think to say The Beatles. They would say the usual answers of 'well, maybe it was the Pope and his visit to Poland in the 1980s.' Some Republicans might say that it was Ronald Reagan and the build-up of the US military that bankrupted the Soviet Union. And this idea of The Beatles, it is just fascinating (*that they were*) a contributing factor."[193]

We have a great responsibility to use our creative gifts wisely. You may think you are just doing what comes naturally, or maybe you do not think what you do is important. But it is! You will influence others by what you create. Whether you choose to do this in a positive or a negative way is up to you.

Art can witness of God

The idea that the arts could originate from the world of the supernatural poses many interesting questions. For example, if it is true, it means that regardless of what an artist's beliefs are, they are representing the supernatural. It is possible that even an atheist could speak about God in his art without realizing it.

The eastern orthodox theologian, Timothy Kallistos Ware said this: "An abstract composition by Kandinsky or Van Gogh's landscape of the cornfield with birds . . . is a real instance of divine transfiguration, in which we see matter rendered spiritual and entering into 'the glorious liberty of the children of God.' This remains true, even when the artist does not personally believe in God. Provided he is an artist of integrity, he is a genuine servant of the glory, which he does not recognize, and unknown to himself there is 'something divine' about his work. We may rest confident that at the last judgment the angels will produce his works of art as a testimony on his behalf."[194]

The landscape of the supernatural is a safe place for the artist who has integrity and takes his gifts seriously. Of course, there are many valleys and much darkness for the artist that is only interested in projecting its evils. Unfortunately, this type of artist wars against himself because regardless of whether he believes in God or not, he is created in His image, and to create art that promotes this darkness means he goes against the very core of what he was created to be. He may receive accolades for his work, but he will never reach his full potential and find true freedom until he completely surrenders to God's ideas rather than his own.

Success is not measured by how many people admire our work, or by how much money we make. We somehow think that someone who is wealthy or famous for his art must be "doing something right." Yet God's opinion of success is measured by how pleased we make Him when using our gifts.

What will last?

We know from our study of the Bible that the world will one day fade away. Yet, as we have discussed, the arts could possibly be a lasting supernatural gift. If we aim to bring down the song from Heaven, the picture, the painting, the poem that is possibly spoken in the echoed hallways of the throne room—will that last after the earth is gone? Is it possible we can open our ears to hear what Heaven is saying, and bring it to earth?

If we can do this, can we reveal the heart of the Father to those who cannot see, and forever change their eternity? Would people be drawn to Christ if we sing His song, speak His words, allow His hand to guide the brush or mold the clay? We may never know until we reach Heaven, but I spend my life on the quest of finding out, and delving deeper into the heart of God and His desire to express himself through my art. It would truly be an incredible revelation to reach Heaven and find that they are singing songs that we have been singing on the earth because a composer turned his ear to Heaven to hear the song.

I heard a story of a man who had a vision that he was in the throne room of Heaven, hearing the angels singing a song that he had written and sung on earth. In disbelief, he turned to one of the angels and said: "I can't believe you are singing one of my songs in Heaven!," to which the angel replied, "We are not—you are singing one of ours—we allowed you to hear what we were singing, and you captured it and brought it to earth." Very humbling indeed!

I wonder if I paused, listened more, lived a more quiet life . . . what would I hear? When I close the door on the chaotic world, I hear so much more, and am inspired to create at a different level. I believe God has given us the invitation to meet with Him, not just in our lounge room when we are on our knees, but in His territory. He invites us to walk with Him in the gardens of His Kingdom and to partake in the sounds and sights of what we think are so far removed from us, yet they are so close that it only requires us to stop, quieten ourselves and enter. The gates are open, and so is the scope for our creativity. It is beyond what we can even imagine. We spend so much time just standing at the entrance gate, because we can feel His presence there, and it feels so good, so we stop and rest. But there is so much more! Are we willing to pay the price by sacrificing ourselves and our desires to enter deeper into this place?

Art and religion

You may be wondering if my words mean that you should only produce religious art, or art for the church. One of the greatest tragedies we face in the arts today is that good art and bad art have been divided into the categories of "religious" and "non-religious." This is an age-old problem and possibly one that may last until eternity. Every great artist who loved God and used their gifts to honour Him had this struggle, as we discovered earlier when we discussed Handel, Bach and Luther.

Rest assured, however, that when you desire to have integrity in your work and be the best that you can be, you are worshipping Him. When you love God with all your heart and want to please Him with your life, it does not matter whether you are a plumber or a prince—you are honouring Him with your life. Where you express your gifts does not determine how godly or how anointed you are. (If I may digress for a moment—it was Keith Green who said: "Going to church makes you as much of a Christian as going to McDonalds makes you a hamburger.")

Do not be discouraged if what you create does not fit within the church context. Some people are called to this; some people are called to other streams for their expression. I wish that all art made with a worshipping heart could be expressed within church walls, but the truth is this may never happen. We just have to look at history to see this. But, it may not be where God wants it! He wants us all to be thriving within the local church, but He also wants us to be a witness to people who may never walk into a church, or who have no idea of who He truly is. Your art could be the key in drawing people closer to Him.

One important truth we must grasp is that as God artists we are *all* called to worship Him with our gifts. We are all called to build and love the church. Please allow yourself the freedom to express truly what is in your heart. God will be glorified and will speak through what you offer Him. In fact, watch how the church thrives when we truly walk in the calling we are born for, rather than try to fit the mold.

Steve Turner in his book *Imagine—A vision for Christians in the arts*, says it perfectly: "I do not believe that every artist who is a Christian should produce art that is a paraphrased sermon. A lot of Christian art is for the sake of art. But because art is also a record and reflects the questions and anxieties of the time, I would like to see contributions that reflect a Christian understanding of that time."[195]

Art that lasts

Many of the artists that we now consider as great were not appreciated until several years, sometimes centuries, after their death. The monk Guido of Arezzo, who invented musical notation, could never have comprehended that almost 11 centuries later we would still be using his methods. It was not until late in his life that Handel was recognized as a great composer. Artists Van Gogh or Rembrandt could not have imagined that millions would know their work centuries later. Charles and John Wesley, or Martin Luther probably never grasped in their lifetime the legacy they have left for the church as it now stands. Our world has been radically changed by their contributions.

Creating something that lasts

It is easy for us to become discouraged when our works are not recognized; however, what we are trying to create is not being overlooked. Rather, it is bigger than we are and therefore goes beyond our own life span. We need to consider this when we create and when it feels as if we are being ignored. If we are truly faithful to what God has called us to do, it may not impact during our lifetime. This is because we are building God's Kingdom, and not our own. So, it is in His time frame, it is His agenda. Sometimes we won't understand this and it will be frustrating so we need to remind ourselves that there is a bigger plan that goes beyond our own sphere of time and understanding. Our responsibility is to be faithful with what God asks us to create.

Entrepreneur and pastor T.D. Jakes once said that history defines us better than the present. In other words, do what you believe you are called to do and people will understand eventually.[196]

> Ec 3:11 *If we can begin a work with the future in mind,*
> *we will do what we do with eternity in our hearts.*[197]

We will always be thinking about creating something that lasts, that can make an impact and capture beauty. It will be a disciplined work, it will be refined, and it will certainly make a difference. Sometimes, it even makes history. This may seem overwhelming, and may seem impossible to you, but I believe the focus is right. Enjoy the process and let the future unfold!

The opinion of the great artist

Throughout time, most great artists have been incredible thinkers, yet not everything they said or believed was necessarily true. This has caused confusion because some people elevate artists to the realms of gods and often accept their teachings without realizing that they are human and fallible. Several years ago a well respected Christian, who was loved and admired, admitted to adultery. The Christian world was in shock and I'm not sure that the person's ministry ever truly recovered, possibly because people became mistrusting and confused. Sometimes famous people are expected to be "superhuman"—and when they fall they fall in a big way.

When something like this happens, we often become disillusioned, especially when someone does something we do not agree with. Alternatively, it can be easy to take everything they say and do as the absolute truth, even when they are doing or saying something that appears to be wrong.

The imperfect artist

Throughout history, we see many contradictions in great men and women who did extraordinary things, yet were human and prone to a darker side. Emperor Constantine, who fervently converted to Christianity and built the great city of Constantinople (said to be the center of Christian worship and learning of this era), was unorthodox in his faith. He was passionate about Christianity, often considering himself to be the 13th Apostle, yet he ordered that his own son be put to death, adamant that he did this with God's will. St. Augustine of Hippo's teachings on salvation and grace still feature in western thought, yet he was a man who struggled with lust. Martin Luther led the great Reformation, yet he had anti-Semitic views. (Adolf Hitler, during his war campaigns, backed up his own opinions by quoting Luther.) John Newton who wrote the incredible hymn *Amazing Grace* preached on the evils of Handel's *Messiah*. These great men were not without controversy and they certainly were not perfect, yet they made a huge impact and changed the world for ever.

God often uses imperfect people. What a great example of his amazing grace, that He would allow the flawed yet gifted artist to represent Him, confident in knowing that somehow He would still be glorified. God is not intimidated by our sinful nature. The fact that God will use us, knowing that we may fail in representing Him, is incredible. He is confident that He is bigger than we are, bigger than our art, and He knows that sometimes, in spite of ourselves and who we are, He will shine through.

When you have a desire to do something great, do not wait until you or your work are perfect. Perfection will never happen, and you will never be happy if you live life like this. You must trust that He will use you in spite of your faults. If you have a desire to be creative and use the gifts that He has given you He will use them.

This does not exempt us from living the best life we can possibly live and to face up to what may hinder us from being all we can be. However, it certainly can empower us to be creative in the here and now, rather than waiting until we reach the elusive end of the "yellow brick road" where we imagine that we will be perfect and therefore better qualified to be used by Him.

Everyone's contribution is significant

With this in mind, we need to appreciate that the artists we admire in our own culture will also not be perfect. We need to be gracious towards them. We need the wisdom and experience of the Holy Spirit to help us make right choices. However, most artistic people, whether you understand their lives and art or not, have something significant to offer. We miss the richness of God's gifts in others (regardless of whether they are Christians or not) when we shut down our minds because we do not understand them.

However, this is also why it is incredibly important to be creative in the way God intended us to be. If we are not grounded in His ways, we will be swayed by whatever our culture throws at us. Instead of faith, we have philosophy. Instead of God art, we have humanism. It is so easy to be influenced by what attracts our attention. Nevertheless, if we are confident in Him, we can appreciate other artistic endeavours for what they are, soak up the sweet nectar, and spit out the bones if need be. If our desire is to be like God, the great artist, everything else will align itself to this central point. We will have a reference point by which we can measure everything else.

Author Steve Turner has this to say: "Some art is so obviously and thoroughly inspired by evil that we can't benefit from it at all. Some art leaves us with images that we find hard to erase or words that come back to haunt us . . . we should respect the power of art. We can't let our spirits take any amount of punishment and expect to emerge unscathed. Sometimes we give ourselves permission to watch, listen or read such material because we say it is 'just for a laugh' or 'a bit of fun.' But that usually means that our critical faculties are relaxed, and it is precisely at these times that our thinking can be shaped by ideas that are antagonistic toward faithful living. I think that T.S. Eliot had it right when he concluded that: 'It is just the literature that we read for "amusement" or "purely for pleasure" that may have the greatest and least suspected influence upon us. It is the literature that we read with the least effort that can have the easiest and most insidious influence upon us.'"[198]

Being misunderstood

With each new movement, there were misgivings from the church. Charles Wesley was criticized by the Calvins, the Jesus People were criticized by the church; the church did not understand Christian music, and then as Christian music grew to encompass more artistic styles there were schisms between the different music genres within the church. From the Renaissance to the Baroque era, classical music to rock 'n' roll, traditional worship hymns to southern gospel and contemporary Christian music—this seemingly endless list should convince us that one form of expression is no better or more holy than the other.

For example, today there are many who would deem classical music superior to contemporary pop music. Yet in the 17th century, both Bach and Handel, two of the greatest classical composers, met with much controversy and were not accepted by the church. Why do we accept their music as godly now, yet not other styles of modern music? We should be asking ourselves these questions and be humbled by them to accept a broader view of what is God art.

Our preferences

I believe it is impossible to compartmentalize God's definition for true worship by an artistic style. God is bigger than that. People have tried to put artistic mediums in frameworks they understand before they accept them. When they do this, they become narrow in their thinking and impose personal tastes as the absolute truth when making decisions about what is "good" art and what is "bad" art.

A better way to approach new artistic endeavour is to be sensitive to the Holy Spirit. How does it make us feel? Are we uncomfortable? Is it just personal preference that makes us choose why we do not like something? How can we see beyond the art to get to the heart of what is trying to be expressed?

The importance of the prophetic

We have a responsibility to become prophetic. I believe that we have forgotten the place that the prophetic plays in our lives as creative people. To be prophetic means to listen to the Holy

Spirit, and hear what Heaven thinks about a situation. When we don't understand, we need not pray from a place of frustration that something does not fit our personal preferences, but from a place where we ask God to speak to us of what we can learn from it. God will use anything and anyone to communicate with the people of the earth. If He could use Balaam's donkey, surely He can use anything! Maybe He is trying to speak to us, and because we do not understand we do not listen.

Let me stress that this does not mean we open ourselves to art that has darkness in it. Again, the Holy Spirit as our friend will help us to decide what is appropriate to allow into our hearts and what is not. We will need to be aware of shadowed corners. We will need to approach everything, not just the arts, with the wisdom of God inside of us. If you are new to this approach, it may take you a while before you feel comfortable that you are really hearing the voice of the Holy Spirit, but the more you practice it, the more confident you will become. (Keeping in mind the validation and importance of lining up with the scriptures of course!)

A history marker of a certain time

The arts are more than just a means of expression. Through those who have gone before us, we have an understanding of culture and history of an era. In essence, their art has left a legacy for the Earth. It is not only an expression of beauty, but a marker, a record keeper for their times.

In Asia in the 8th century, Du Fu was considered a "poet historian" because he described military tactics and governmental rule in his historical poems. The monks throughout Europe were meticulous at keeping manuscripts of religious text. Rembrandt was well-known for painting subjects exactly as they were, as opposed to romanticizing them, and in doing so captured the culture of his day. He was often criticized by his peers for depicting ordinary people such as washerwomen, instead of the beautiful goddesses portrayed in some other artists' portraits. Rembrandt painted what he saw in real life. It is because of this we have a true, historic marker of what times were like in his era.

Your art captures a moment in time

When we write a song, a novel, or paint or sculpt, we are capturing a moment in time for those who will come after us. This does not mean that everything we do needs to be heavy and serious. Fun songs, such as *A Hard Day's Night* or *She Loves You* by The Beatles may not seem to say anything of great importance to us today, but they captured a culture, a moment, a feeling that many can relate to. These songs represented a huge change in musical style, and were a snapshot of the lifestyle of the day.

Art reflects a point in history. When people think of certain songs, they remember a moment in time. The songs become the bookmark of a person's life. Just think about a song for which you have fond memories. When you hear it, you remember a certain moment in your life. Maybe it was a love song shared by you and your partner, a poem written for a child's Christening, or a piece of classical music played at your grandfather's funeral.

When you create, keep this in mind. Try to capture something that is worth keeping. Something worthy of any generation claiming it as their own. Bob Dylan and Paul Simon are admired by generations that have followed them because they write music that is relevant to all humankind. That is the kind of art that will last.

The church's struggle

My studies reveal that there were only two occasions throughout history where the arts significantly thrived from within the church. Between the 14th and 17th centuries in the Renaissance era, the Catholic Church would commission artists to paint or sculpt works that would decorate their buildings, or the houses of rich patrons. As the church of this era gave freedom to the artist to be creative, and provided a financial means for them to focus on their art, it thrived.

This kind of freedom was seen again in the 1970s, with the Charismatic renewal. When artists were given freedom to explore the reaches of their gifts, they flourished. The benefit to the church has been extraordinary. In both periods in history when art thrived in the church, we see growth in all aspects of the church. There are churches around the world today that have allowed this freedom, and the health, effectiveness and vibrancy of their congregations are evident.

Boundaries and freedom

One might think that this means that the artist should be given complete freedom to do whatever they want. This is not so. When the Catholic Church commissioned their artists to provide them with art, there were expectations as to what was wanted. An example can be found in the 16th century, when musician Louis Bourgeois was commissioned from within the Calvin Church to put the Psalms to music. There were immense restrictions put upon him to complete the works to specific requests in line with the church's beliefs. Although this could have ended in frustration for Bourgeois, what was created was a beautiful work called the *Genevan Psalter*. It is rich and simple in spite of the strict boundaries put upon it.

Alan Wilson-Dickson says: "Sometimes artistic inspiration and sheer necessity come together to produce something exceptional. To suggest composers need a free reign to create what their inspiration dictates is a romantic fiction. On the contrary, practical restrictions are absolutely necessary to provide a framework for creativity."[199]

Thus, we see a balance between boundaries and freedom. In fact, leadership of the artist from within the church is an important topic. When a creative person is surrounded by the right people they can soar and thrive, but when an artist feels restricted they will suffocate. Within the Charismatic Movement or the Renaissance, we see that artists were given a framework for what was needed, yet they were also given the freedom to be expressive. It takes a great leader to allow this balance in an artist's life within the context of the church arena. Many creative people are misunderstood, which leads to them being rejected within the church. This is a great loss, both for the church and the artist, and we need to do all we can to protect this from happening.

What these moments in history also show is that God will reveal himself, regardless of freedom or restrictions. Bourgeois had rules to follow before he could complete his work; the Catholic Church commissioned artists to create and then left them to do it; Handel did not create work from within the church framework, yet today his music is accepted by most church denominations; Martin Luther's folk songs were common tunes with gospel lyrics and were looked down upon by many. Yet all of these artists have contributed to making the church what it is today. Again, we see that God will use anything and anyone to speak to us. He will be heard!

What this means for you

As an artist, maybe you feel you have restrictions imposed upon you. Know that God will still move. Be faithful to the gift that is in you and watch how He uses it. We spend so much time looking at the problems that surround us that we forget to invest in our gifts. If we can focus on how we can use our gifts and how we can improve them, we will be more productive.

Instead of trying to push our way through, the gift itself will make room.

Pr 18:16 (NIV) *A gift opens the way for the giver and ushers him into the presence of the great.*

The NKJ version translates:

A man's gift makes room for him and brings him before great men.

The initial idea of this scripture was that you could bribe the great by appeasing them with a gift. This gift would then make a way by softening the heart of the recipient. If we concentrate on presenting something beautiful, we can open up people's hearts! This scripture is as true today as it was when it was written. Instead of looking at the circumstances around you, look inside yourself. What is God saying to you? What does He expect you create? What does He want? Follow that and it will lead to great works of art that will not only stand the test of time, but will go beyond any limitations that man can put upon you. In doing so, God will reveal Himself through your gift to the world.

26

Conclusion

I never wanted to be famous. I only wanted to be great.[200]
Ray Charles

Sometimes you struggle hard to feed your family one way, you forget to feed them the other way, with spiritual nourishment. Everybody needs that.[201] James Brown

I'm not saying I'm going to change the world, but I guarantee that I will spark the brain that will change the world.[202] Tupac

To use our artistic talents wisely and passionately is to embrace the heart of God. Our gifts become arms that reach out to Him. When people are searching for Him, even though they may not understand, they will write about Him, paint Him, and act Him out, even despite their unbelief. It can lead others to Him, even if that was not the intention of the artist. I believe this is because God as the great artist who created art will inevitably shine through any artistic expression, because it is at the core of who He is.

If we are created in His image, then His DNA is on the inside of us regardless of our spiritual leanings. There is a connection to Him whether we recognize it or not. Of course, many things can prevent this from happening, but an honest heart will always attract the attention of God. He will use every opportunity to romance his people back into His arms. Whether that be to speak through a donkey as He did in the Old Testament, or through the rock singer who is still searching for answers and is unsure of the existence of God, He will find a way. This is evidence in itself of how creative God can be.

I believe the quest to understand the supernatural will be further explored through artistic mediums. This means it is vital that we as God artists sift through it all to find the power behind what we believe in, and to express that in a powerful way that can impact the searching heart. It is not enough for us to know the truth—we must search for the truth. We must dig deeper than the surface of what we inherently know as Christians. There is more treasure in the soil than we could ever imagine:

> Col 2:2–3 *My purpose is that they may be encouraged in heart and united in love, so that they may have the full riches of complete understanding, in order that they may know the mystery of God, namely, Christ, in Whom are hidden all the treasures of wisdom and knowledge.*[203]

> Is 45:3 *I'll lead you to buried treasures, secret caches of valuables—Confirmations that it is, in fact, I, God, the God of Israel, who calls you by your name.*[204]

This is a moment in history where if we are wise with our talents we can be more than just a great singer or a great songwriter. We can be more than a talented artist or author. We can become signposts on the road for truth for a still relevant, saving Gospel.

When we are passionate about the right cause and put it into our art, just like St. Augustine, Luther, Handel, Bach or U2, we can change the world for ever, and the world will be better because of it.

Let the God artist arise!

Endnotes

Chapter 1 Introduction

1   www.quotegarden.com

Chapter 2 God as the great artist

2   www.quotegarden.com

3   Message Translation

4–5   New International Version

6   www.crosswalk.com—online Old KJV Hebrew Lexicon

7   Dake, F.J. (1963) *Dake's Annotated Reference Bible*. Dake Bible Sales Inc., Lawrenceville, Georgia, USA

8   *Trials turned to God*. Keith Green, from the album *For him who has ears to hear*

9   www.meaningoflife.i12.com/body.htm

10   www.cafeoflifepikespeak.com/amazing%20Facts.htm

11   news.bbc.co.uk/1/hi/sci/tech/2748653.stm Universe to expand forever, by Dr. David Whitehouse, BBC News online science editor

12   *Indescribable* DVD, Louie Giglio

Chapter 3 The artist and discipline

13   L'Engle, M. (1980) *Walking on Water: Reflections on faith and art*, Harold Shaw Publishers, Wheaton, Illinois, USA.

14   Dr. Albert Schweitzer

15–17   New International Version

18   Elsheimer, J. (2001) *The Creative Call: an artist's response to the way of the spirit*, WaterBrook Press, Colorado Springs, Colorado, USA, page 20

19–20   The Message

21   L'Engle, M. (1980) *Walking on Water: Reflections on faith and art*, Harold Shaw Publishers, Wheaton, Illinois, USA, pages 106–107

Chapter 4 The artist and forgiveness

22   Elsheimer, J. (2001) *The Creative Call: an artist's response to the way of the spirit*, WaterBrook Press, Colorado Springs, Colorado, USA, page 54

23   The Message

24   Demoss, N.L. (2006) *Choosing Forgiveness*, Moody Publishers, Chicago, USA

25   www.merriam.merriam-webster.com

26   Demoss, N.L. (2006) *Choosing Forgiveness*, Moody Publishers, Chicago, USA

27   The Message

28   New International Version

29   The Message

30   New International Version

31   The Message

32–33   New International Version

Chapter 5   Artists as prophets

34   Kavanaugh, P. (1992) *The Spiritual Lives of the Great Composers*, Word
         Publishing, Milton Keynes, England, page 146

35   Kramarik, A. and Kramarik, F. (2006) *Akiane: Her Life, Her Art, Her Poetry*,
         W Publishing Group, Nashville Tennessee, USA, page 71

36–37   Dake, F.J. (1963) *Dake's Annotated Reference Bible*. Dake Bible Sales Inc.,
         Lawrenceville, Georgia, USA

38   New International Version

39   Perez, P., *The Prophetic Worshipper*, e-book from www.jasperstonemusic.
         com

40   Ira Milligan (2000) *Understanding the Dreams you Dream: biblical keys for
         hearing God's voice in the night*, Destiny Image Publishers, Shippensburg,
         Pennsylvania, USA

41   www.passionforjesus.org/developingthepropheticinworship.html

42–47   New International Version

46   Perez, P., *The Prophetic Worshipper*, e-book from www.jasperstonemusic.com

47–61   New International Version

Chapter 6   The artist and the tabernacle—our role as priests

62–63   New International Version

64   Roberts Liardon, (1996) *God's Generals*, Albury Publishing, Tulsa,
         Oklahoma, USA, page 86

65   Exodus 25: 10–22, Ark of the Covenant

Chapter 7   The artist and the priesthood—our role as priests

66   www.quotegarden.com

67   New International Version

68   Joyner, R. (1996) *The Surpassing Greatness of His Power*, Morning Star
         Publications, Charlotte, North Carolina, USA, page 94

69   The Message

70–71   New International Version

72   The Message

73–75   New International Version

76   Hayford, J. (2005) *Manifest Presence—Expecting a Visitation of God's Grace
         through Worship*, Chosen Books, Michigan, USA, page 115

Chapter 8   The artist, DNA and the power of sound

77   www.brainquote.com—Mike Figgis, film director, writer and composer

78   www.brainquote.com—David R. Brower, environmentalist

79   *The Creative Spirit* CD series, John Paul Jackson, Streams Ministries International

80   Morris, H.M. (1976) *The Genesis Record: A scientific and devotional commentary on the book of beginnings*, Creation Life Publishers, San Diego, California, USA

81   Dan McCollam DVD (2007), School of the Prophets Conference, Prophetic Declaration session, Bethel Church, Redding, California, USA

82   New International Version

83   http://en.wikipedia.org/wiki/Susumu_Ohno

84   news.nationalgeographic.com/news/2005/10/1021_051021_protein_music_2html National Geographic article: Your DNA is a song—scientists use music to code proteins

85   Dossey, L. www.nyu.edu/classes/neimark/music.htm

86–88   New International Version

89   Dan McCollam DVD (2007), School of the Prophets Conference, Prophetic Declaration session, Bethel Church, Redding, California

90   *The science behind music—the principle of entrainment* www.vth.biz/kb/index.php?article=50
        Sound feelings—the entrainment transformation principle www.soundfeelings.com/products/alternative_medicine/music_therapy/entrainment.htm

91–92   New International Version

93   Pierce, C.D. (2002) *The Worship Warrior—How your prayer and worship can affect your home and community*, Regal Books, California, USA, pages 202–203

94   New International Version

95   A great book on this topic is *Worship evangelism—inviting unbelievers into the presence of God* by Sally Morgenthaler, Zondervan Publishing House, 1995

96   New International Version

Chapter 9   The artist and the world

97   Markee, David (1995). *The Lost Glory*, Morning Star Publications, page 15

98   New International Version

99   Turner, S. (2001) *Imagine: A vision for Christians in the arts*, InterVarsity Press, Downers Grove, Illinois, USA

100–102 New International Version

Chapter 10   Introduction

103   www.wisdomquotes.com

Chapter 11   In the beginning

104   www.thinkexist.com

105   www.brainyquote.com

106   New King James Version

107   New King James Version

108   New International Version

109   The Message

110   Riedweg, C. (2008) *Pythagoras: his life teaching and influence*, 2nd edition, Cornell University Press, New York, USA

111–112 Wilson-Dickson, A. (1997) *A brief history of Christian music*, Lion Hudson, Oxford, UK, page 57

113   Navia, L. (2007) *Socrates: a life examined*, Prometheus Books

114   Havelock, E. (1963). *Preface to Plato (Volume 1) History of the Greek mind*, Belknap Press of Harvard University Press, Cambridge, Massachusetts, USA

Chapter 12   Bible times

115   www.quoatationspage.com Mary Angelou, famous US author and poet

116   Dake, F.J. (1963) *Dake's Annotated Reference Bible*, Dake Bible Sales Inc., Lawrenceville, Georgia, USA

117   Wilson-Dickson, A. (1997) *A Brief History of Christian Music*, Lion Hudson, Oxford, UK, page 26

118–120 New International Version

121   Wilson-Dickson, A. (1997), *A Brief History of Christian Music*, Lion Hudson, Oxford, UK, page 33

122   Blainey, G. (2000) *A Short History of the World*, Penguin Books, Australia

123   Wilson-Dickson, A. (1997) *A Brief History of Christian Music*, Lion Hudson, Oxford, UK, page 38

124   Ferguson, G. (1966) *Signs and Symbols in Christian Art*, Oxford University Press, USA

Chapter 13   The early church

125   www.ccel.org/ccel/schaff/npnf109.xix.xiv.html Saint John Chrysostom, church father, biblical interpreter and Archbishop of Constantinople, 347–407

126   www.quoteworld.org

127   Hughes, R. (2000) *Sound of Heaven Symphony of Earth*, Morning Star Publications, page 118

128   Schaeffer, Frances A. (2005) *How should we then live?* Crossway Books, USA, page 26

129   *The Confessions of St. Augustine* (2005), Modern English Version, Baker Books, Grand Rapids, USA

130   Schaeffer, Francis A. (2005) *How should we then live?* Crossway Books, USA, page 31

Chapter 14   Art around the world and the Dark Ages

131   www.worldofquotes.com Flaccus Albinus Alcuinus, teacher, scholar and poet

132   Schaeffer, Francis A. (2005) *How should we then live?* Crossway Books, USA

Chapter 15   The rise of the arts once again

133   www.thinkexist.com

134   Schaeffer, Francis A. (2005) *How should we then live?* Crossway Books, USA, pages 51–52

Chapter 16   The Renaissance

135–137 www.brainyquote.com

138   Schaeffer, Francis A. (2005) *How should we then live?* Crossway Books, USA

139   Jeffares, A.N, (1997) *The Critical Heritage*, Routledge, UK, page 294

140   http://undpress.nd.edu/book/P00898/Notre Dame Press, Indiana, USA

141   Schaeffer, Francis A. (2005) *How should we then live?* Crossway Books, USA page 60

142   *Leonardo DaVinci/The Divine Michelangelo* DVD—2004 BBC Worldwide Ltd

143   Schaeffer, Francis A. (2005) *How should we then live?* Crossway Books, USA, page 60

144   *Leonardo DaVinci/The Divine Michelangelo* DVD—2004 BBC Worldwide Ltd

145   Schaeffer, Francis A. (2005) *How should we then live?* Crossway Books, USA, page 51

Chapter 17   The Reformation

146–147 www.xristos.com/pages/quotes_page.htm

148   Schaeffer, Francis A. (2005) *How should we then live?* Crossway Books, USA, pages 80–82

149   www.Christianhistoryinstitute.com Glimpses #154. *Highlights of Luther's life in his own words*

150   Wilson-Dickson, A. (1997) *A Brief History of Christian Music: From biblical times to present*, Lion Hudson, Oxford, UK, page 93

151   Wilson-Dickson, A. (1997) *A Brief History of Christian Music: From biblical times to present*, Lion Hudson, Oxford, UK, page 100

152   Wilson-Dickson, A. (1997) *A Brief History of Christian Music: From biblical times to present*, Lion Hudson, Oxford, UK, pages 101–102

153   Schaeffer, Francis A. (2005) *How should we then live?* Crossway Books, USA, pages 87–92

Chapter 18   The Baroque era

154   www.thinkexist.com

155   Schaeffer, Francis A. (2005) *How should we then live?* Crossway Books, USA, pages 41–42

156   Taken from *Novum Organum Scientarium*, Schaeffer, Francis A., *How should we then live?* (2005)

157   Kavanaugh, P. (1992) *The spiritual lives of great composers*, Word Publishing, Milton Keynes, England, pages 27–34

158   Kavanaugh, P. (1992) *The spiritual lives of great composers*, Word Publishing, Milton Keynes, England, pages 17–24

159   http://w3.rz-berlin.mpg.de/cmp/handel.html Handel

Chapter 19   Romanticism and science

160   www.thinkexist.com

161–162 www.brainyquote.com

163   Kavanaugh, P. (1992) *The spiritual lives of great composers*, Word Publishing, Milton Keynes, UK, page 57

164   Wilson-Dickson, A. (1997) *A Brief History of Christian Music: From biblical times to present*, Lion Publishing, Oxford, UK, page 185

Chapter 20   Realism collides with Romanticism

165   www.whatquote.com

166   www.brainyquote.com

167   Hughes, R. (2000) *Sound of Heaven, Symphony of Earth* Morning Star Publications and Ministries, Charlotte, North Carolina, USA

Chapter 21   Science and the computer age

168   www.brainyquote.com

169   www.xristo.com

170   www.wesselenyi.com and www.wesselenyi.com/top100books.htm

171   Various authors (2003) *Spiritual journeys: How faith has influenced twelve music icons* Relevant Books, Lake Mary, Florida, USA

172   http://en.allexperts.com/q/Dylan-Bob-448/Rock-Hall.htm

173   Still on the Road, Second Gospel Tour 1980

Chapter 22   The emergence of the Christian music industry (CCM)

174–175 www.brainyquote.com

176   www.jesuspeoplemovement.com
Di Sabatino, D. (1999) *The Jesus people movement: An annotated bibliography and general resource*, Greenwood-Heinemann Publishing, Santa Barbara, California, USA

177   www.larrynorman.com

178   Larry Norman (1972) *Why should the devil have all the good music?* From the album *Only visiting this planet*

Chapter 23 Contemporary Christian music and the rebirth of church worship

179 www.brainyquote.com

180 Wilson-Dickson, A. (1997) *A brief history of Christian music: From biblical times to present*, Lion Publishing, Oxford, UK, pages 412–416

181 www.christianmusicplanet.com

182 Information collated during conversations with Christian media mogul Wes Jay (www.woodlandsmedia.com)

183 Her book *Extravagant Worship* is a *must* read for worshippers!

Chapter 24 The arts today and passion for the supernatural

184 Blainey, G. (2001) *A Short History of the World*, Penguin Books Australia Ltd, Victoria, Australia

185 www.christianitytoday.com Pentecostal Te Sequel, April 2006

186 Various authors (2003) *Spiritual Journeys: How faith has influenced twelve music icons*, Relevant Books, Lake Mary, Florida, USA, page 245

187 Various authors (2003) *Spiritual journeys: How faith has influenced twelve music icons*, Relevant Books, Lake Mary, Florida, USA, pages 202–204, quoted from Tracey Pepper, "Deep joy" interview, July 1998

188 Various authors (2003) *Spiritual journeys: How faith has influenced twelve music icons*, Relevant Books, Lake Mary, Florida, USA, pages 132–133

Chapter 25 What we can learn from the past

189 www.quotegarden.com

190 Jeremy S. Begbie (2000) *Theology, Music and Time*, Cambridge University Press, New York, USA, page 76

191 New International Version

192 www.contemporarywriters.com

193 http://transcripts.cnn.com/TRANSCRIPTS/0309/13/lkl.00.html (Larry King Live—quote by Richard Shenkman in a panel discussing Paul McCartney's first trip to Moscow, September 13, 2003

194 Allchin, Rev Cann A.M., Sobornot—from the magazine *Sobornost*, quoted from the book *Walking on Water* by Madeline L'Engle

195 Turner, S. (2001) *A Vision for Christians in the Arts*, InterVarsity Press, USA

196 Hillsong Conference 2007

197 New International Version

198 Turner, S. (2001) *A Vision for Christians in the Arts*, InterVarsity Press, USA, page 42

199 Dickson, A.W. (1997). *A Brief History of Christian Music: From biblical times to present*, Lion Hudson, Oxford, UK, page 153

Chapter 26   Conclusion

Bibliography

Books

Assayas, M. (2005) *Bono on Bono: Conversations with Michka Assayas*, Hodder and Stoughton, UK.

Blainey, G. (2001) *A Short History of the World*, Penguin Books Australia Ltd, Victoria, Australia.

Brinkley, D. (2003) *Almanac of World History*, National Geographic Society, Washington DC, USA.

Bryson, B. (2003) *A Brief History of Nearly Everything*, Doubleday, UK.

Bynun, J. (2005) *The Threshing Floor: How to know without a doubt God hears your every prayer*, Charisma House, Lake Mary, Florida, USA.

Cameron, J. (1993) *The Artist's Way: A course in discovering and recovering your creative self*, Pan Books, London, UK.

Conner, K.J. (1976) *The Tabernacle of David* Bible Temple—Conner Publications, Portland, Oregon, USA.

Dake, F.J. (1963) *Dake's Annotated Reference Bible*, Dake Bible Sales Inc, Lawrenceville, Georgia USA.

Demoss, N.L. (2006) *Choosing Forgiveness*, Moody Publishers, Chicago, USA.

Elsheimer, J. (2001) *The Creative Call: an Artist's response to the Way of the Spirit*, WaterBrook Press, Colorado Springs, Colorado, USA.

Fergusson, A. (2005) *Songs of Heaven: writing songs for contemporary worship*, Hillsong Church Ltd, New South Wales, Australia.

Hibbert, V. (1999) *Prophetic Worship: releasing the presence of God*, Cuington Press, Dallas, Texas, USA.

Hughes, R. (2000) *Sound of Heaven, Symphony of Earth*, Morning Star Publications and Ministries, Charlotte, NC, USA.

Hughes, T. (2003) *Passion for Your Name: resourcing worship leaders—refreshing worshippers*, Kingsway Communications Ltd, Eastbourne, UK.

Joyner, R. (1996) *The Surpassing Greatness of His Power* Whitaker House, New Kingston, Pennsylvania, USA.

Joyner, R. (2002) *Breaking the Power of Evil*, Destiny Image Publishers Inc., Shippensburg, Pennsylvania, USA.

Kavanaugh, P. (1992) *The Spiritual Lives of Great Composers*, Word Publishing, Milton Keynes, UK.

Kramarik, A. and Kramarik, F. (2006) *Akiane: her life, her art, her poetry*, W Publishing Group, Nashville, Tennessee, USA.

L'Engle, M. (1980) *Walking on Water: Reflections on faith and art*, Harold Shaw Publishers, Wheaton, Illinois, USA.

Marshall, S.M. (2004) *Restless Pilgrim: The spiritual journey of Bob Dylan*, Relevant Media Group, Orlando, Florida, USA.

Morgenthaler, S. (1995) *Worship Evangelism: Inviting unbelievers into the presence of God*, Zondervan Publishing House, Grand Rapids, Michigan, USA.

Morris, H.M. (1976) *The Genesis Record: A scientific and devotional commentary on the Book of Beginnings*, Creation-Life Publishers, San Diego, California, USA.

Noland, R. (1999) *The Heart of the Artist; A character-building guide for you and your ministry team*, Zondervan Publishing House, Grand Rapids, Michigan, USA.

Noland, R. (2004) *Thriving as an artist in the Church: Hope and help for you and your ministry team*, Willow Creek Association, Grand Rapids, Michigan, USA.

Peacock, C. (2004) *At the Crossroads: Inside the past, present, and future of contemporary Christian music*, WaterBrooke Press, Colorado Springs, Colorado, USA.

Pierce, C.D. (2002) *The Worships Warrior: How your prayer and worship can protect your home and community*, Regal Books, California, USA.

Roberts, J.M. (1995) *History of the World (3rd edition)*, Penguin Books, London, UK.

Di Sabatino, D. (1999) *The Jesus People Movement: An annotated bibliography and general resource*, Greenwood-Heinemann Publishing, Santa Barbara, California, USA.

Schaeffer, F. (1981) *Addicted to Mediocrity: 20th Century Christians and the arts*, Crossway Books, Wheaton, Illinois, USA.

Stockman, S. (2001) *Walk On: The spiritual journey of U2*, Relevant Books, Lake Mary, Florida, USA.

Turner, S. (2001) *Imagine: A vision for Christians in the arts*, InterVarsity Press, Downers Grove, Illinois, USA.

Various authors (2003) *Spiritual Journeys: How faith has influenced twelve music icons*, Relevant Books, Lake Mary, Florida, USA.

Various authors (2005) *Restoration of the Tabernacle of David: Preparing the way for the King of Glory*, Progressive Vision Publishing, Jerusalem, Israel.

Wilson-Dickson, A. (1997) *A Brief History of Christian Music: from biblical times to present*, Lion Publishing, Oxford, UK.

Zschech, D. (2001) *Extravagant Worship*, Check Music Ministries, Castle Hill New South Wales, Australia.

DVDs

Leonardo/The Divine Michelangelo—2004 BBC Worldwide Ltd.

CDs

The Creative Spirit series—John Paul Jackson, Streams Ministries International.

Quantum Physics, Music and the Prophetic CD series—Bob Jones, Ray Hughes, JoAnn McFatter, David Van Koevering, The Elijah List.

Other

Message Translation

New King James Version

New International Version

Index